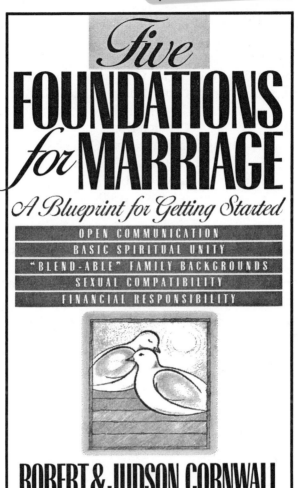

Five FOUNDATIONS *for* MARRIAGE

A Blueprint for Getting Started

OPEN COMMUNICATION
BASIC SPIRITUAL UNITY
"BLEND-ABLE" FAMILY BACKGROUNDS
SEXUAL COMPATIBILITY
FINANCIAL RESPONSIBILITY

ROBERT & JUDSON CORNWALL

Creation House
Lake Mary, Florida

Copyright © 1991 by Robert Cornwall
Printed in the United States of America
Library of Congress Catalog Card Number: 90-81610
International Standard Book Number: 0-88419-283-0

Creation House
Strang Communications Company
600 Rinehart Road
Lake Mary, FL 32746
(407) 333-0600

Unless otherwise noted, Scripture quotations are from the
New King James Version of the Bible. Copyright © 1979,
1980, 1982 by Thomas Nelson Inc., publishers. Used by
permission.

Second printing, August 1991
Third printing, January 1993

To Shirley Mae, wife of Robert,
and to Eleanor Louise, wife of Judson—
our companions, confidantes and colaborers
in the ministry for almost half a century

ACKNOWLEDGMENT

We wish to express our appreciation to Dr. Dianne McIntosh for writing the worksheets for this book. In the Ken and Kathy sketches, she has shared her years of experience as a professional counselor. The self-examination tests are taken from tests used regularly in her ministry. Her contribution is a labor of love to the body of Christ.

Thank you, Dianne.

CONTENTS

PREFACE

Marrying the living and burying the dead are inescapable ministries for all pastors. During my years in the clergy, I (Robert) have done my share of both. At the moment I can't see the long-term effect of the way I've buried the dead, but I can see the effects of many of the marriages I've performed. Even as a young pastor I learned that the kind of flowers, the number of candles or the size of the wedding party had nothing to do with the strength of a marriage. Even the liturgy I used was all too soon erased from the minds of the bride and bridegroom. The wedding, however sacred, was but a ceremony and a celebration. Sometimes there wasn't much to celebrate a few years later.

I soon saw the value of premarital counseling; a fence at the top of a cliff is superior to a hospital at the bottom. Like many other pastors, I now refuse to perform a wedding ceremony for a couple with whom I have not had opportunity to do such counseling.

In my early pastoring, I found considerable good literature available. But over the years I developed my own counseling pattern that was both practical and easily visualized by a couple so emotionally involved that words seldom penetrated the haze.

Other pastors, hearing of this material's success, have borrowed it for use in their congregations. At the strong urging of others, I made it available on video tapes from which audio tapes were duplicated, as couples often wanted to review what they had been told before the wedding. Then I was asked to put the material in book form. At this point I was stymied, for Robert Cornwall is not a writer. Fortunately, my brother, Judson, is, and he volunteered to work with me. As the book unfolded, he added material from his own broad counseling experience, and we chose to release the book as jointly authored.

Together we have spent more than ninety years building our marriages. We offer our experience to all who are married or who are considering the prospects.

Robert Cornwall
Scottsdale, Arizona
1990

CHOOSING
A LOCATION

In a House or on
the Street?

I (Robert) was raised in a parsonage, and, since I entered the pastoral ministry directly from college, I began raising my family in church-owned houses. Over the years I resented having to ask permission to repaint a room or remove a plant from the yard. The annual church budget dictated whether a worn carpet could be replaced, and personal whims of committee members determined the color scheme with which I was forced to live. Only someone who has lived in institutionally owned facilities can understand the elation I felt when I took the pastorate of a church that preferred giving me a housing allowance over owning and maintaining a parsonage. My immediate response was,

"I'll build myself a house!"

Between this expressed desire and the actual moving day, we spent months planning, purchasing, pounding nails and painting. Finding money for the ambitious dream proved to be the small end of the project. We had to choose the section of town in which we wanted to locate; then we needed to find a building lot within our budget. Once these choices were made, we had to settle on house plans. My wife and I pored over building plans for weeks until we found a floor scheme and an exterior design we both liked.

We invested months in decision making before the first tree in the filbert orchard was cut down to make room for my dream.

Building the house was the fulfillment of a long-term desire, but I have never again taken the time to repeat the process. In subsequent moves I've purchased an existing home, and I've discovered that many of the principles I learned in the advance planning of constructing a house apply equally in preparing to purchase a building.

I see parallels between my housing experience and marriage. You and I were born into the marriage house of our parents, and we lived our first twenty or so years there with them. In most cases, that living situation was adequate, but that house was theirs and not ours. As we matured, we wanted to build our own marriage house. Having our own ideas of the floor plan we wanted, the structural style that would suit us and the landscaping we would enjoy, we set out to have a marriage of our own.

Much of what I learned about building a house applies to the building of a marriage too. Location is important. If you want to raise horses, it's probably unwise to marry a man who loves the city life. The deeply devout man will find it difficult to build an effective marriage with an atheistic wife. The saying goes that the three most important rules for success in business are location, location and

12

location. Could this also be true of marriage? You're going to live in this marriage for the rest of your life. Is the location sufficient to stand the test of time?

The plans are almost as important as the site. The arrangement of rooms and the exterior style of the marriage should be tailored to fit the needs of the persons moving into that marriage house. Furthermore, those plans should allow for some flexibility, because plans for marriage are plans for a family. The two who enter the marriage often multiply, and room must be made for those additional persons.

While not all decisions can be made in advance, most of the determining choices should be finalized before taking the sacred vows of marriage. It is far easier to change the architect's plans before construction than after the concrete is poured and the walls are erected.

Pastors and real estate agents often observe similar patterns of behavior in individuals. Some persons approach the purchase or construction of a house deliberately and carefully. They come informed. Others respond emotionally to a style, color or location. They put money down almost immediately, without much thought. What takes some people months, others do in moments. Similarly, some people approach marriage with caution, consideration and care, while others give it less serious consideration than the purchase of an automobile.

Purchasing a house and entering into marriage have at least five similarities. Each requires a *reason,* introduces a *responsibility,* inspires an expected *return,* involves some *risk* and demands frequent *repairs.* Far too frequently, people enter into these long-term contracts without sufficient advance thought and preparation.

Reasons

The *reason* for home ownership varies with individuals. Some people purchase a house for an investment and others for prestige, but most buy a house to have a place to live. They want to make that house into a home. Similarly, people approach marriage for diverse reasons. Some do so for sexual convenience, others for business purposes, but the majority approach marriage as a life-style. Here they will make a home. The relationship is the primary source of needed security, comfort and companionship.

Few people purchase a house expecting to lose it. Yet thousands of homeless people live on the streets of our cities. Many of them once owned comfortable houses, but poor planning, failure to work their plans or circumstances beyond their control snatched away their main investments. Similarly, our divorce courts are overloaded with people who entered into marriage full of dreams and hopes. Now they await the dissolution of their marriages, which puts them out on the streets emotionally. Sometimes the contract is broken because it was entered without sufficient preparation. Other times the couple fails to have a plan to preserve the marriage. Frequently the failure is simply the result of not following through with the plan previously set. Occasionally the failure is the result of outside forces over which the couple has little or no control.

Responsibilities

A marriage contract, like a real estate contract, introduces a distinct *responsibility*. In either case, the down payment is small compared to the total cost. Just as monthly house payments must be met year after year, so a consistent investment is necessary to maintain a marriage. Irresponsibility in meeting contractual agreements will bring foreclosure on a house and divorce in a marriage. The mortgage on a house might extend over thirty years, but the payments on a marriage last an entire lifetime. The heavy responsibility gets even greater as children arrive.

Returns

No one would take on such responsibilities unless something inspired an expected *return.* Just as the purchase of a house is probably the largest investment most of us will ever make, and just as it will likely become our greatest asset, so marriage is the most valuable personal commitment most of us will make—aside from our acceptance of Jesus Christ as personal Lord and Savior. Marriage promises us more security, joy and emotional stability than any other relationship. Just as a house usually appreciates in value through the years, so a marriage becomes more valuable in time. As I've often said, young love may be exciting, but old love is very comfortable.

Risks

Marriage and home ownership both involve *risks.* Occasionally the value of real estate depreciates over the years, leaving the homeowner with more debt than equity. Even though the contract requires continuing payments, there may come a day when there's no income. Foreclosure is one risk of home ownership, but it's not the only risk.

Sometimes the house turns out to be less desirable than first thought. It may have serious defects that went unnoticed in prepurchase inspections. I once bought a house without requiring a termite inspection. (The seller told me that his brother-in-law, an inspector, had assured him he saw no evidence of termites in the house.) When the kitchen floor began to sag, the sad truth unfolded. My unfounded trust cost me several thousand dollars.

During the early years of a marriage, people frequently discover that a spouse does not fully measure up to expectations. While courting, two people often try to be what they think the other wants, but in marriage each sees what the other actually is. As one woman put it, "Love is blind, but marriage is an eye-opener."

Lifetime relationship pledges always involve risks. While there are no money-back guarantees, there are ways to lessen the risks before entering into marriage, and there are ways to repair damages to a marriage after the "termites" are discovered.

People who want to wait until the marriage risk factor is zero had better learn to live alone. Life is ever changing, and people change with it. The challenge can be exhilarating or exhausting and destructive to the union. A couple's expectation of perfection and complete safety in marriage is as unrealistic as the expectation that mortgage payments on a house will always be convenient and easy to make. How do you proceed? Wisely calculate the risks involved, do your best to lessen them, and learn to live with any negatives that arise.

Repairs

Any homeowner or spouse of several years will attest to the need for frequent *repairs*. Happy is the homeowner who is handy with tools, for the earlier a repair is made, the less it costs. Similarly, the sooner repairs are made in a marriage, the less costly they will be. Though marriage isn't hardware, it receives hard wear. Marriage is the blending of two individuals into a single working unit. Conflicts in interests and clashes of wills can flare into flames of emotion. Words said in anger can leave deep wounds that, if not healed quickly, infect the entire marriage. Far too many divorces are the result of accumulated little damages that were never corrected. Even a well-built home will disintegrate if it isn't properly maintained. A well-adjusted marriage can fail unless the partners are willing to mend the breaches and repair any destruction that comes either from within or without.

Our Purpose

The purpose of this book is to help individuals preparing for marriage understand the reasons for marriage; accept the responsibility they're facing in making this decision; know what to expect out of marriage; calculate the risks involved in this decision; and understand the need for frequent repairs in the relationship.

A secondary purpose is to help married couples evaluate the state of their marriages and perhaps gain some fresh insights on how to strengthen and freshen their commitments.

May the subsequent chapters of this book become a maintenance list for married couples as well as a blueprint for those contemplating the "plunge." Throughout we will compare a marriage with the building of a house, for even the Bible says, "First the natural and then the spiritual." As we progress, we'll discuss looking at the plans, selecting and preparing the lot and laying the foundations. It takes a lifetime to build the marriage house, and if these initial steps are done correctly, the house is likely to stand the storms of life and reflect the individuality of those who built it.

Worksheet

Ken and Kathy met in church, fell in love and are now planning to marry. Recent college graduates, they both love the Lord and are beginning their separate careers.

Kathy's bachelor's degree is in business, and she's a management trainee at a local bank. She's hoping to work her way up in the company.

Ken also has a bachelor's degree in business. Employed in the personnel department of a small manufacturing company, he has hopes of eventually managing the company.

As they're talking one day over lunch, Ken and Kathy encounter their first major conflict. The subject of children is raised, and Ken, who came from a large family, says he wants to have a large family—the sooner the better. Kathy, an only child, says she wants no more than two children, and only later in life.

1. From this scenario, which of the following or other reasons may be motivating each spouse-to-be to marry:
- to satisfy ego needs
- to provide a reason for leaving home
- to provide companionship and alleviate loneliness
- to guarantee financial security
- to have children
- to be with the one loved

2. How does each person view his or her partner's eventual family responsibilities?
- A husband's ideas for his wife may be:
  - to be a mother who works just until she gets pregnant.
  - to be his companion in sexual fulfillment.
  - _____.

- A wife's ideas for her husband may be:
  - to be a source of security for the family.
  - to be a lover and defender.
  - _____.

3. How would you help this couple resolve their differences of opinion; understand why each feels the way he or she does; agree on a realistic approach to the timing and number of children?

ONE

LOOKING AT THE PLANS

So You Want to Get Married?

"It is not good that man should be alone;
I will make him a helper comparable to him."
—Genesis 2:18

In his best-selling book *Business by the Book* (Nelson, 1990), financial counselor Larry Burkett tells of moving his organization into a leased building a few years ago. Unfortunately, he soon discovered the building had serious problems.

"The contractor had failed to prepare the foundation properly," Burkett writes, "and the building began to sink into the soft foundation below it. As we sat in our offices, we would suddenly hear the walls crack and feel the building settle another inch or so. Our decision to relocate our materials shipping department to the upper floor caused the settling to accelerate. Visitors to our offices would panic at the sounds emanating from the building, fearing an earthquake was striking. The front sidewalks eventually stood four to six inches above the building entrance!" (p. 9).

What a work environment! But that's what can happen when a building isn't constructed properly, beginning with the very foundation. To help you lay the proper foundation for marriage, we start in this chapter by looking at the nature of the institution from God's perspective and then at some practical ways to prepare for this closest of all human relationships.

The urge to settle down with a lifetime companion has finally overwhelmed you. You're certainly not alone in this desire. In the United States alone, more than two million couples say "I do" each year. Although the customs and ceremonies vary widely, all cultures practice marriage. It's certainly in order for you to join the ranks of humanity who live two-by-two instead of single file.

The concept of marriage may seem scary, and many today call it silly or stupid, but it actually is sacred. God's Word declares, "A prudent wife is from the Lord" (Proverbs 19:14). And a prudent husband is God's gift as well. Marriage is God's provision to humanity for procreation, for help in life's difficult spots and to alleviate loneliness.

Marriage has its beginnings in God Himself. The Bible begins with the story of creation. When all was complete, God created Adam to have dominion over everything. God made Adam for His own purpose and pleasure and in His own image. Placed in the special garden of God's creation, Adam enjoyed a unique fellowship with God as they walked and talked together in the cool of the day. Adam was the student, and God was his only teacher. This relationship was fulfilling to God, but He recognized it wasn't completely fulfilling to Adam. God observed, "It is not good that man should be alone; I will make him a helper comparable to him" (Genesis 2:18).

God put Adam to sleep, took a rib from his side and formed Eve. Certainly God could have created Eve from the dust of the ground in the same way Adam was created. Nevertheless, He took something out of the man and used it to create his helpmate. A part of Adam was in Eve.

Man was created in the image of God. The stamp of God's nature and character was upon him. However, when God formed Eve, some of those characteristics of our heavenly Father became dominant in the woman, while others remained dominant in the man. When God presented Eve to Adam, the man's response was,

This is now bone of my bones
And flesh of my flesh;
She shall be called Woman,
Because she was taken out of Man.

To this God added, "Therefore a man shall leave his father and mother and be joined to his wife, and they shall become one flesh" (Genesis 2:23-24).

Those traits of the Father that were once found all together in Adam were now shared with Eve. Though neither one was devoid of any aspect of God's image, yet certain aspects of God's image were perfected in Adam, and others were perfected in Eve. Each of them sensed the other had something desirable and even needed.

A desire for marriage is a confession of incompleteness. The strong macho male often longs for the tenderness that escapes him. He finds it in a proper relationship with his wife, while she finds in him the strength she desires. Marriage enables each person to complete the other. God designed it this way.

FIVE FOUNDATIONS FOR MARRIAGE

So You've Purposed to Get Married?

It's one thing to want marriage as a life-style, and quite another to purpose fully to get married. Those who merely wait and believe that "it will happen" often live frustrated, lonely lives. Marriage is not a disease that some catch while others remain immune. Marriage is the result of a decision that is pursued to a definite end.

Although God provided marriage as a channel for the completion and fulfillment of individuals, He does not command anyone to get married. He highly recommends it, but He doesn't require it. Both married and unmarried persons were used of God in the Scriptures. In the first letter to the church in Corinth, the Holy Spirit spoke through Paul commending both marriage and celibacy (see 1 Corinthians 7). There's much to be said for the single life, and likewise much to be said for marriage. But the admonitions we write in this book are for those who have chosen to marry.

Obviously, the first step toward marriage is finding a partner. Solomon, who "had seven hundred wives, princesses, and three hundred concubines" (1 Kings 11:3), wrote, "He who finds a wife finds a good thing, and obtains favor from the Lord" (Proverbs 18:22). Again, this is equally true of the woman who finds a good husband.

Note the two action verbs in that proverb, *finds* and *obtains*. Solomon didn't find most of his wives. They were princesses given to him for political alliances. They turned his heart away from God in his older years. Mere companionship with the opposite sex does not enable us to find favor with God; it comes as we search for the partner who will balance our lives.

In Christian circles it's common to hear people say, "I'm just waiting for the marriage partner God will send to me." It can become a lifelong wait! If we're ready to marry, we should be looking patiently but actively for a mate. Through creation God has provided a pool of men and women from which we make a choice, but the decision is always ours. To widows the Word says, "She is at liberty to be married to whom she wishes, only in the Lord" (1 Corinthians 7:39). If a widow on her second-go-around has the right of personal choice, certainly the person facing a first marriage has the same privilege. The single scriptural limitation in choosing a partner for life is "only in the Lord." (We'll discuss this in a later chapter.) Ask God for guidance, but don't expect to be divinely compelled.

Finding a partner is not a weekend activity. A lifetime commitment deserves a studied search and lots of prayer and should not be merely an emotional choice. I've known people who give more attention to their choices of automobiles than to the choice of a mate. Since you'll spend the rest of your natural life with your spouse, get to know someone before making a commitment. Sometimes the cute little mannerisms that initially grab your attention will drive you crazy in the long haul of marriage. The primary goal of marriage should not be excitement but long-term compatibility. Make your choice accordingly.

If you're seeking your partner, don't look where you wouldn't want to live. Even if you liked a house in Minneapolis, you wouldn't buy it if your job and interests were in Los Angeles. If you don't want a drinking mate, don't look for your mate in a bar. If you want a Christian companion, don't look for him or her in the non-Christian world. Marriage does not automatically and immediately change a person's life-style. Ask yourself if the life-style of the person in whom you're interested is one you could share comfortably for the rest of your life.

Are You Willing to Prepare for Marriage?

If you have sincerely purposed to marry, isn't it about time to prepare for marriage? I don't mean prepare for the wedding but for the life that follows the ceremony.

Our great American universities train students for a variety of careers. Though they prepare young and old to take their place in the social and economic world, they do nothing to prepare students for marriage. Choosing a lifetime companion is a far more serious decision than choosing a career, but the choice is usually made with little or no advance preparation. We mistake a strong biological urge for maturity, but marriage is far more complex than simple sexual union.

How do you prepare for marriage? Read some good books on the subject. Talk about marriage with married friends. Practice accountability in handling money. Start a savings account, and deposit at least 10 percent of your earnings, since a ready cash flow is needed at the start of marriage. Plan your purchases for your future home. The "hope chest" can be very practical. Many small appliances needed in the first home can be secured while you're in the preparing-for-marriage stage. I have known young men with the foresight to purchase small houses rather than rent apartments. Later, when they asked the women of their dreams to leave their fathers' homes to become their wives, they had places to take them.

Experiment in putting the desires of another above your own. Youth is a time of great self-centeredness, but marriage is sharing. Learning to give unselfishly of yourself before committing to marriage is excellent preparation.

Visit a retirement center or a rest home. Share some of your dreams and energy with those people. You'll be surprised at how much wisdom they can give you in return. Volunteer for service in the children's department of your church to get a feel for being with children. Remember that plans for marriage are usually plans for a family. How do you really feel about children?

Many young people don't realize the day-to-day work involved in domestic life. Discipline is important on every hand. Breadwinners must go to work on time whether or not they feel like it. The cook needs to get food on the table whether or not he or she is in the mood.

Though cooking and housekeeping are generally thought of as women's roles, I'm grateful to my mother for teaching all her sons how to do those things. They have certainly come in handy. Men, your wives will not always be at your beck and call. A wife is not a maid. I've seen too many men who didn't know how to operate a washer and dryer! For both sexes, the domestic chores you learn now won't have to be learned later.

Practicing the meaningful art of communication with the opposite sex will also help you plan for a successful marriage. Good communication is a learned experience— not an automatic gift imparted during the wedding ceremony. Gentlemen, you may have a good rapport with the fellows, but can you talk with women? They don't always think the way guys think. Ladies, men have difficulty talking about their feelings, while it may seem natural to you. A good brother-sister relationship is a great asset here, but if you don't have one, you can practice on others— maybe at church, work or school.

Anything that increases your maturity level will help prepare you for marriage. Break out of the usual mode and do something different. Few things broaden life's horizons better than travel. Increase your education. This will give you more knowledge, and it will enhance your social graces.

About ten years ago, while ministering in England, I (Judson) met a recent convert from the streets of London. A group of believers was discipling her in the ways of the

Lord. Her love for Jesus impressed me, but I observed that she was socially withdrawn. Since she headed the small drama team for the crusade at which I was speaking, she had to talk with me daily to find my theme for the evening, hoping to adjust their drama presentation to coordinate with the message.

By the end of the week, I realized she wanted to break out of her small English world but didn't know how. She jumped at my suggestion that she come to America. It took a year of working through her local church fellowship to convince her leaders that this was wise and probably from God. When all were in agreement, she flew to the United States, and I enrolled her in a Bible school. It was an entirely different world for her, but she blossomed like a plant transplanted into a garden from a greenhouse.

After graduation she married the top student in her class, and they, with their three daughters, are now missionaries in Indonesia. It took this travel and change to prepare her for a totally different life from that which she had lived before.

In marriage you will be giving yourself to another. Do you know what you have to give? Get acquainted with yourself. Are you comfortable with what you find?

No matter how far along you are in your plans to get married, you and God still have time to improve the person you will be when you marry. Those persons who have the most luck in their careers are the best-prepared people. "Luck" is usually little more than being ready to move with opportunities. The same principle applies to marriage. A good match isn't so much a matter of finding Mister Right or Sister Wonderful as it is being prepared to present yourself to that person when you do meet.

"An excellent wife is the crown of her husband" (Proverbs 12:4). An excellent husband is equally the crown of his wife. Obtaining this king or queen of mates requires an excellent choice.

Woruksheet

Ken and Kathy were glad for their first conflict (about children), because it took the veil off their "romantic love." They could begin to see each other honestly.

To continue their preparation for marriage, Ken and Kathy listed their own liabilities (bad points) and assets (good points), and then they listed their mate's liabilities and assets.

After half an hour, Ken and Kathy compared lists. Ken was very upset when he saw that his good point of "leadership" was on Kathy's liability list as "bossy."

How do you see yourself? Do you see that your greatest strengths can also be your greatest liabilities? How do others see your strengths? Kathy saw Ken's strength in leadership as it affected her, and it became a liability.

We have included a questionnaire to help you understand what you see in yourself and how you see your prospective mate. Make photocopies so each partner can fill one out. Then discuss why you answered as you did and which traits you see as strengths and which as weaknesses.

How I See You and Me

Put a check next to the words that describe you or your partner.

You	Partner	
_____	_____	Tender
_____	_____	Creative
_____	_____	Materialistic
_____	_____	Fun
_____	_____	Loving
_____	_____	Parental
_____	_____	Quiet
_____	_____	Spiritual
_____	_____	Assertive
_____	_____	Aggressive
_____	_____	Strong
_____	_____	Talkative
_____	_____	Loyal
_____	_____	Compassionate
_____	_____	Others-centered
_____	_____	Jealous
_____	_____	Romantic
_____	_____	Lazy
_____	_____	Reliable
_____	_____	Attentive
_____	_____	Consistent
_____	_____	Unappreciative

_____	_____	Manipulative
_____	_____	Faithful
_____	_____	Hardworking
_____	_____	Truthful
_____	_____	Stubborn
_____	_____	Intuitive
_____	_____	Callous
_____	_____	Honest
_____	_____	Gentle
_____	_____	Restricted
_____	_____	Generous
_____	_____	Self-centered
_____	_____	Accusative
_____	_____	Pushy
_____	_____	Ambitious
_____	_____	Possessive
_____	_____	Emotional
_____	_____	Sensitive
_____	_____	Passive
_____	_____	Unreasonable
_____	_____	Egotistical
_____	_____	Logical
_____	_____	Organized
_____	_____	Rigid
_____	_____	Inconsistent
_____	_____	Playful
_____	_____	Strong-willed
_____	_____	Despondent

TWO

SECURING
THE LOT

Do You Know What
You Are Getting Into?

"Consider your ways!"
—Haggai 1:7

Some time ago, I enjoyed a sumptuous meal in a restaurant built around a huge, live ponderosa pine—I mean right in the middle of the building and up through the roof. Admiring it, I told the manager, "What a novel idea!"

"Novel? Nuts! It's nasty," he replied. "It was a bad idea. Every ant in the area comes down the tree to plague the customers. The squirrels run through it. Besides, the tree still grows, but the building doesn't. Trees are trees and buildings are buildings, and the two of them should never be married together like this."

He was right, of course. Beyond the novelty was the

inconsistency of it all. The tree's life was threatened because it was so difficult to water, and the building was threatened by the constant growth of the tree.

Clearly, the architect and builder should have thought through all of the ramifications of building around a tree. They didn't see what they were getting into. Do you know what you're getting into in contemplating marriage? From our years of experience with premarital counseling, we can predict your answer.

Your first response is likely, Yes! Of course I know what I'm getting into. I've thought this through, and the two of us have spent hours talking about our future.

But are you sure? If we were face to face, we would probably detect a hint of hesitancy and uncertainty on your part. Marriage incorporates the lure of the unknown, which, although it is fascinating, is equally fear producing.

Marriage is a lifetime commitment between two people who should be in love. Marrying to "fix" problems—social or selfish, emotional, family pressure, or even pregnancy—should never be considered. Marriage is for those who have found a comfortable and fantastic relationship of love.

In parts of the world where matches are still arranged by parents, some people declare that marrying for love is part of the decadent Western culture. But in those same places, the role of women is usually lowered. They're often viewed as little more than slaves. The Bible teaches that love is the glue that bonds two different people into a working unit. It's the blender that causes distinctive differences to be so homogenized as to produce a new entity. When a "he" and a "she" bond in a loving marriage, they produce a "they."

God's Word does not leave love as an option in marriage. Four times Paul commanded husbands to love their wives. In his letter to the Ephesians he wrote:

"Husbands, love your wives, just as Christ also loved the church and gave Himself for it.... So husbands ought to love their own wives as their own bodies; he who loves his wife loves himself....

"Let each one of you in particular so love his own wife as himself, and let the wife see that she respects her husband" (Ephesians 5:25,28,33).

To the church in Colosse Paul added: "Husbands, love your wives and do not be bitter toward them" (Colossians 3:19). These are not suggestions, but commandments.

You may well ask, What is love? We wish we could tell you. Love is many different things. Someone has described it as a lizard you can't catch, although it runs up and down your spine. Someone else has defined it as an itch on the inside that you can't scratch—though somebody else can. Both of these metaphors are concerned with the emotional aspect of love. We've heard people married for many years describe love as time. They're not far off the mark, for it takes a lot of time to truly love.

One of the best ways to find out what we love is to see where we spend most of our time. When two are preparing for marriage—in love—it's amazing how much time they can find to talk, phone or just be together. Love involves an investment of time.

We would also suggest that love is value. The older we get, the more we see that love is interrelated with a value system. Let us illustrate what we mean: I (Robert) have an automobile, and I also have an old Jeep that I use when I go hunting. If I found my car with a flat tire, I'd change the tire carefully, making certain I didn't scratch the car in any way. If I found the old Jeep with a flat tire, however, I'd be likely to kick it in the side and growl at it! The only difference is value. Both vehicles are means of transportation, but one is far more precious to me than the other. And so it is with love. One person, one human relationship, is more valued than any other. The longer you're married, the more you invest in each other, giving all you have. This makes the marriage very valuable and worth protecting with your life.

Another person experienced in love may well say that love is caring. Love is compassion and being tenderly involved with one another. Love demands involvement; you can't love without doing. Love is sharing, giving of yourself. The greatest marriages we have observed are bonds between people who aren't trying to see what they can get out of the marriage but what they can put *into* the relationship. Matrimony is give and take, and it should always be in that order.

Marriage Is a Composite

Even before exchanging the marriage vows, ask yourself, What do I intend to put into this marriage? What do I expect to get out of this marriage? You need to come to grips with what marriage is to you. Is it a source of sex? Yes, of course it is. Is it a spiritual fulfillment? It can be. Is it companionship? Yes, that's also involved. But you and your chosen partner ought to sit down and start talking about what you're willing to invest in this marriage and what you plan to get out of it, for anticipations pretty much determine our fulfillments. When we don't get what we expect, we're not fulfilled. Any relationship has to do with what we do and what we expect to get in return for that deed. What we expect to get determines what satisfies us. With your intended spouse, openly discuss the issues: Here is what I expect to give to this marriage, and this is what I am expecting to get out of it.

There's a complexity to love, this key ingredient to marriage. We've seen that love is an involvement, an emotion, a sense of value, a caring and a sharing. But love cannot be properly defined apart from God, for "God is love" (1 John 4:16).

Even then, love is difficult to explain. Perhaps an illustration would help. We see love as being a tossed green salad. It begins with lettuce alone. (That's the honeymoon ingredient—let us alone—get it?) Then you add some tomatoes, a radish or two, perhaps a bell pepper, some mushrooms, a little onion and a grated carrot for color. You put this all together and mix it up with a lot of highly flavored dressing and say, "Here's a tossed green salad." If you take your fork and pick out the mushrooms, the onions, the bell pepper, the radishes and the lettuce, you no longer have a salad. It is salad only when it's heaped together and stirred up. In the same way, when you start to isolate individual things in love and say, "This is love or that's love," you may have the ingredients for love, but you don't have love. All the ingredients need to be stirred together with a tasty emotional dressing to make a presentable salad of love.

By now you may be wondering, Why in the world are you advising us on marriage if you can't tell us what love is? Actually, our limitations are worse than that, for we can't even tell you what marriage is supposed to be, since every marriage is a bit different. There are some very emotional, "loud" marriages, punctuated by yelling, and yet those two people genuinely love each other to the core. Then there are the formal marriages, where it seems the spouses don't touch each other without wearing gloves. There are also those very "hot" relationships in which partners make love every day. We don't know which marriage you aspire to have, and we may have left out your specific category, but we can share some general principles about marriage— what it is and what foundations will make it strong.

Marriage Is a Covenant

Marriage is far more than two consenting adults living

together. It goes beyond a legal contract or an agreement. The biblical concept of marriage is a covenant relationship. The English language has no good synonym for *covenant,* the only word that properly covers marriage.

The Bible itself is a covenant made by God. Our canon of Scripture is divided into the Old and New Covenants, or Testaments. Within those are additional covenants into which God entered with individuals and with the Jewish nation.

The Bible also records lesser covenants made between individuals. Those early Jewish covenants had at least seven articles of agreement in them:

1. The covenant partners were acquaintances who often knew each other well and held a deep, abiding esteem for each other, such as David and Jonathan.

2. The covenant partners often held all things in common. The property of one was considered the property of the other.

3. The covenant was always struck before witnesses.

4. The parties to this covenant made exchanges with each other as symbols of taking on the other's identity. This trading of belts, robes or weapons was viewed as a binding together of the two.

5. The parties offered an animal sacrifice.

6. The covenant partners usually exchanged names.

7. The partners celebrated a covenantal meal with each other.

That Jewish concept of a covenant is a clear illustration of the Judeo-Christian concept of marriage:

1. Marriage belongs to friends, not to strangers.

2. In marriage all things are held in common: "With all my worldly goods, I thee endow."

3. Marriage is entered in the presence of witnesses.

4. The partners exchange strengths, symbolized in the exchange of rings.

5. The life of another is shared in sexual intercourse.

6. There's an exchange of names.

7. A covenantal meal is celebrated in one form or another.

Covenants are lifelong. An American Indian custom from the movies demonstrates what a covenant should be. The old Westerns often incorporated a scene where the white man and the red man joined together to go on a rescue mission of some sort. Ceremonially drawing their hunting knives, they would slice their wrists or make a cut in their palms and then hold the wounds together so that their blood would mingle. This made them blood brothers.

That's what happens in a Christian marriage. The husband and wife in covenant together become one. As they join in sexual union, they consummate a covenantal relationship. The Scripture says that he who joins himself with a harlot is joined to her in heart and spirit, because the sexual union is the cutting of a covenant. There is no marriage without that sexual relationship.

Every time we deal with God, we are responding to a covenant-making God. God made a covenant with the first couple. When Adam and Eve violated that covenant, they lost their right to the Garden of Eden. Similarly, in a marriage, a breaking of the covenant terms is costly to both parties.

God always keeps His covenants, and so He commands that we keep the covenant of marriage. If we're faithful to our vows, marriage will provide the fulfillment of life that He intended. However, when one part of the marriage covenant is broken, pain, tension and penalty are introduced (though the partnership need not break up). If healing is to come to that broken relationship, forgiveness must prevail. As God has proved to us, covenants do work under the banner of forgiveness. So should marriage.

As you recognize that your marriage is a covenant,

remember that this is the second greatest covenant you will ever enter. The most important, of course, is choosing Jesus Christ as your Lord and Savior. That commitment parallels marriage all the way through the Scriptures. For example, "Husbands, love your wives, just as Christ also loved the church and gave Himself for her" (Ephesians 5:25). "Come, I will show you the bride, the Lamb's wife" (Revelation 21:9).

Building a Marriage

A good marriage doesn't just happen. It must be built. Compare the building of a marriage with the construction of a house. Before work can begin, you must secure a piece of property—a lot. In a marriage the lot is your love, as love precedes marriage.

A house is not normally constructed at one site and then transported to the lot; it's built on the lot. Similarly, you can't pull your marriage out of the sky and park it on someone else's property. Your marriage is a house, not a house trailer. If, indeed, love is a lot, you'll need a lot of love. Even after securing that lot, you may find it overgrown. There may be a rosebush or a former boyfriend bush. There's the huge "mama" tree, and the "daddy" tree may shade the whole property. What will you do about the things already on your lot? You could bring in a bulldozer and tear out everything, but every lot needs room for both the marriage-house and the proper relationships of the past. You need not cut off all your past relationships, but you do have to build your marriage around and in conjunction with them.

In addition to your mother tree and father tree, you may also have a sister or brother tree, and those trees can't be bulldozed out just because you're preparing to build a marriage-house. But you can construct your marriage with those trees in your yard and not in the middle of the building (remember the restaurant mentioned at the beginning of the chapter). Every house is enhanced by trees in the landscape.

Some bushes definitely *should* come out—the former girlfriends and boyfriends. If they remain a part of your life, they will be occupying the spot on which your house is to be built. It's nearly impossible to build around them; you need space for your marriage to be constructed.

You can have any kind of house you desire—split level, ranch style, large, small—but the structure cannot be bigger than the lot, and it's wise to leave room for some shrubs. A marriage shouldn't monopolize all your love.

So now we have the lot (your love), and we have the plans for the house (your marriage). You may think that's the end, but it isn't. It's only the beginning.

All houses, and all marriages, have foundations. While we haven't told you exactly what love is and we can't tell you precisely what marriage should be, we *can* tell you what the foundations of your marriage have to be. That's what this book is about: the five foundations of marriage. Every exterior wall of a house has to have a foundation of one sort or another, and every support-bearing interior wall requires an additional foundation. Likewise with marriage.

We may tend to think that one of those foundations for marriage is more important than another, but that's not true. The most important foundation in a marriage is the one that's sinking, cracking or crumbling—the one that no longer holds up its share of the load. Similarly, the most important part of your car is the part that isn't working! If your carburetor is working correctly, you don't think about it. But if the carburetor isn't doing what it's supposed to, it gets all your attention. The same is true for any part of your automobile, whether it be the engine, the tires or the radiator.

So it is with the five foundations of marriage. It's not

that one is more important than the others, but if one isn't working, it becomes our top priority. Sometimes it's relatively easy to see that something isn't quite right on the homefront. It may be harder, however, to pinpoint the problems. Not knowing what to do, we do what someone else suggests. We bring in the flowers, the candy and the second honeymoon; but those only aggravate the problem because we have merely tried to alleviate the external evidence of a crumbling foundation. We use cosmetics when we should use construction. Candy has never solved a marriage problem. Flowers have never taken care of a need. They may open a door for communication, but corrective action is needed for the sagging house of a marriage to be made straight and level.

The five fundamental foundations for a marriage are: communication, spiritual harmony, family background, sexual compatibility and money. All are important; healthy marriages have a majority of them.

Worksheet

Ken and Kathy visited their pastor to make decisions about their wedding. He asked each of them to fill out a questionnaire detailing his or her personal habits and those of the partner.

When Ken and Kathy compared the results, they were surprised they still didn't know each other as well as they thought. But they had fun discovering new aspects of one another.

Following is a questionnaire on personal habits and qualities. Again, make photocopies for each of you. Fill one out as well as you can. Share them with each other and your pastor in your premarital counseling.

Personal Habits and Qualities

Listed below are some questions that will help you understand more about each other as a couple. Sometimes small differences and expectations can build up huge walls between you. Have fun as you go through this list. Answer each statement as it applies to you and then as you think it applies to your partner. Then share it with your future spouse!

You	Partner	
_____	_____	How many hours a week do you spend watching TV?
_____	_____	Do you snore when you sleep?
_____	_____	Does bad breath bother you?
_____	_____	Do you like to cook?
_____	_____	Do you fall asleep watching TV or movies?
_____	_____	Do you leave your toenail clippings lying around?
_____	_____	Do you pick your nose?
_____	_____	Are you a borrower?
_____	_____	Do you like to read before you go to sleep?
_____	_____	Do you hide things under the bed?
_____	_____	Do you smack your lips when you eat?
_____	_____	What time do you usually go to bed?

_____	_____	Do you cry at sad movies?
_____	_____	Do you wish you were organized?
_____	_____	Are you cheerful when you wake up?
_____	_____	Are you stingy?
_____	_____	Do you normally wash your own clothes?
_____	_____	Are you a soft touch for a sad story?
_____	_____	Do you eat fast?
_____	_____	Do you stay in bed when you have a cold or a slight case of the flu?
_____	_____	Are you a helper?
_____	_____	Do you take medication regularly?
_____	_____	Do you lay things down as soon as you walk in the house?
_____	_____	Do you plan your days off?
_____	_____	Do you often leave your shoes lying around?
_____	_____	Do you give to charity?
_____	_____	Do you keep your car clean?
_____	_____	Do you like to watch the news?
_____	_____	Do you like to grocery shop?
_____	_____	Do you like to be shown affection in public?

_____	_____	Do you enjoy watching people?
_____	_____	Can you balance a checkbook?
_____	_____	Do you regularly do the dishes?
_____	_____	Do you like to eat snacks?
_____	_____	Do you burp?
_____	_____	Do you floss your teeth?
_____	_____	Do you bite your nails?
_____	_____	Do you like to eat in bed?
_____	_____	Do you lose your keys often?
_____	_____	Are you a lender?
_____	_____	Are you a day or night person?
_____	_____	Are you a picky eater?
_____	_____	Do you sing in the shower?
_____	_____	Are you often late?
_____	_____	How many hours of sleep do you need?
_____	_____	Do you squeeze the toothpaste from the middle?
_____	_____	Do you swear or curse?
_____	_____	Do you consider yourself a private person?
_____	_____	Do you keep your room clean?
_____	_____	Are you a perfectionist?
_____	_____	Do you have a cup of coffee to wake you up?

_____	_____	Do you clean the bathroom sink after using it?
_____	_____	Do you like to be in charge?
_____	_____	Do you wear pajamas?
_____	_____	Do you think a man should change a baby's dirty diaper?
_____	_____	Do you like to go to parties?
_____	_____	Do you enjoy yard work?
_____	_____	Do you like to shop for clothes?
_____	_____	Do you enjoy holidays?

THREE

THE FRONT ELEVATION

Have You Established Lines of Communication?

"The tongue of the wise promotes health."
—*Proverbs 12:18*

A building must have a foundation for its outside walls plus foundation blocks for the floor joists. Any architect will tell you that a building cannot be any stronger than its foundation, and most builders will say that one should be prepared to spend up to one-third of the cost for the house on the foundation.

Years ago when my brother and I were building a church in Kennewick, Washington, we were criticized for the size of the footing we poured and for insisting that we reinforce it with steel. Few other buildings being erected in that area were doing this.

Today that church structure still stands without cracks in

its block walls, while other buildings constructed at the same time have been torn down or repeatedly repaired. You see, whether we are erecting a building, developing a spiritual life or entering a marriage relationship, there is no substitute for a strong foundation.

For the front elevation of a marriage, the essential foundation is communication. This foundation needs to be dug deep and firmly reinforced, as all areas of the relationship depend on how well the spouses get their messages across to each other. Most of the marital problems we counselors see stem from poor communication.

Communication is almost a lost art. One reason for this is the misconception that saying words is communication. Our generation has been overpowered with words. Words are everywhere—on signs, on blaring radios. Television invades the eye and ear with emotional words intended to motivate and manipulate. As a subconscious defensive measure, our minds begin to block out those media messages. The same thing can happen in a marriage. Having so much to talk about, we become insensitive to the volume of words exchanged.

Don't get me wrong. We need words to communicate. Nonverbal communication is a healthy supplement to, but no adequate substitute for, spoken communication.

The Art of Listening

Contrary to popular opinion, the art of listening is more basic than the art of speaking. You listened before you spoke. When you first spoke, you imitated what you'd heard and seen. And a healthy adult maintains the physical ability to hear and see. If we cease to use our abilities as fully as we once did, it's usually because we're so busy talking that we forget to listen.

For about three years, my wife and I (Robert) lived on a

small farm a few miles from the church I was pastoring. The farm gave our family a needed relief from parsonage life. One morning I rushed into the house after feeding the cattle, intent on taking a fast shower before heading to the church. As I rushed through the kitchen, I gave several instructions to my wife, Shirley, who followed me into the bedroom saying something about the car. Almost simultaneously, I told her that our pregnant Jersey cow looked as if she could give birth at any time.

The noise of the shower drowned out further conversation. A few minutes later, when I stepped out of the bedroom dressed for the office, I couldn't find Shirley anywhere. I rushed to the garage, only to find my car missing!

Returning to the kitchen, I picked up the keys to Shirley's car and returned to the garage. Her car wouldn't start. I was furious! I had an important meeting in less than fifteen minutes with the architect who was supervising the construction of our new church structure. I phoned my secretary to send someone out to get me.

That evening I exploded at Shirley for stranding me. "But, Bob," she said, "I told you my car wouldn't start and that I had a dental appointment. Weren't you listening?"

No, I wasn't. I was talking and thinking about the cow. Needless to say, I ate humble pie for dessert that night.

Good communication involves listening to a *person*, not merely to words. In themselves, words are only tools of communication. What we seek to convey is far more important than the conveyance itself. You quickly discover this when trying to talk with someone who is deaf or someone who doesn't understand English. With body language, hand gestures and facial expressions, we communicate thoughts without the help of words.

Similarly, feelings such as anger, love, happiness and dissatisfaction can be expressed in verbal *and* nonverbal manners. Unfortunately, we listen only to words—to the exact word instead of exactly to the person. Husbands and wives: learn to listen to the person speaking more than to the choice of words used.

It's easy to choose a wrong word without realizing what you've done. For a public speaker, this can be embarrassing. While speaking at a funeral, a pastor, intending to say, "This mortal shall put on immortality," actually said, "This mortal shall put on immorality." Though the pastor's heart said the right thing, his mouth said it incorrectly. What might have destroyed the solemnity of the funeral didn't do so, however, as the family was listening to the *person* and understood his intent.

Similar poor choices of words frequently occur between a husband and wife. That's why it is so important to listen for underlying thoughts rather than merely to words. To paraphrase Jesus: listen as you would like to be listened to. Try to get into the speaker's mind to think with him or her. Why is the speaker saying this? What does he or she feel? What has provoked this line of communication? Am I hearing overtones from on-the-job pressures or parental frustration? Good listening will qualify the words used in the communication.

Have you ever known people who listen with what we call a "stutter mind"? While you're talking, you can tell they're thinking, Yes...but,...yes...but,...yes...but. You know you're not the most important thing on their minds. Their response to you is occupying center stage.

When another person is speaking, concentrate your energies on hearing him or her rather than on formulating your answer. Your time to speak will come. Then you can stop and think before you answer.

When a partner is talking about problems, it's easy to say, Oh, I don't want to hear about this! But cookie crumbs under the rug call ants and roaches as easily as cookie crumbs out on a counter. A wise spouse knows that problems don't go away just because they're hidden. Open communication is crucial.

When communication breaks down between a husband and wife, a referee may be needed. In a counseling session, the mere presence of a third party can help us hear what is really being said. As sad as it may seem, many husbands and wives come to like each other better after their divorce than during their marriage; the divorce lawyers taught them how to speak up and to listen to what their mates were saying. Sadly, we've heard many husbands and wives say, "Now that I've divorced her (or him), I really like her. While we were married, I wish we could have talked the way we did during the divorce proceedings." How tragic that we often have to come to a crisis before we learn to communicate.

The Art of Talking

The fact that a partner is a good listener is no excuse, however, for sloppy communication, giving inaccurate facts and being dishonest about our emotions. The Bible commands us, "Do not let the sun go down on your wrath" (Ephesians 4:26). Since we have no control over the setting of the sun, this command must be concerned with how we handle our anger. Denying it is not acceptable, as one party would be going to bed angry with the other. Settling the anger demands communication—speaking and listening.

Anger-resolving discussions are not opportunities to pick a fight, either, but times to pursue peace. "Why do you always...?" is one of the most dangerous phrases for a spouse to utter.

I (Robert) love to play golf. If I could do so, I would golf every day. Of course this is impossible, but my days off frequently find me playing in a foursome on one of the many courses in my area. As you might guess, this is not always compatible with my wife's plans for our day together.

I well remember one week when we were enjoying beautiful weather. Wednesday night after church, Shirley and I decided to pack a picnic lunch the next day and drive out of town to a special park we enjoy. We had kept a heavy schedule for several weeks, so we decided to sleep in, have a late breakfast and perhaps leave the house about 10:00 a.m.

I am a morning person for whom sleeping in is very difficult, however, and I woke with the dawn on Thursday and just couldn't make myself lie in bed any longer. So I got up thinking I would read, but the crisp morning air begged me to play a fast nine holes at the closest golf course. Leaving a brief note on the refrigerator door telling Shirley I would be back by nine, I headed for the course. While drinking a cup of coffee in the club house, three doctors invited me to play with them. Naturally, I accepted. Their fellowship was enjoyable on the front nine, and I felt I was making a valuable contact for future pastoring opportunities. Thus, when they insisted I join them on the back nine as well, I stayed with them.

It was past noon when we finished the eighteen holes. Refusing their invitation to join them in lunch, I rushed home, stopping enroute to pick up a bouquet of roses. I walked into the house with a silly grin on my face and said, "These are for you, honey."

Shirley shocked me by throwing the flowers on the floor and shouting, "Where were you? You promised that we would have today together! You always do this to me!"

"Always?" I responded. "When was the last time I did something like this?"

To my amazement, she knew almost to the day.

"But that isn't always," I said. "I've lost track of time on the golf course a few times, I admit, but not always."

I knew I was wrong in what I had done. Obviously, she felt rejected, but she hurt me when she said that I always do this. The argument that followed totally erased any plans for the picnic. Instead, we endured a day of tension while I worked in the yard and she got her oils out and painted a picture.

How do you respond when someone says, "Why do you always do such and such?" I'll bet you come back with, "I do *not* always do that! I've done it once or twice (or perhaps five times in the past year), but I do not *always* do that!" Or what about an accusing, "It's just like you to do (or say) that!" Unwittingly, the speaker has slandered the character of the accused. Equally bad is the opening statement, "Why don't you act (or talk or whatever) like so and so?" Comparison with another is demeaning and unnecessarily introduces a third party into a private discussion. Consciously avoid the accusing "You always..." and "Why do you...?"

Solutions come much more easily when we talk about our emotions. Rephrasing the issue, "When you do (or say) that, I feel like...," brings the conversation to your own emotions while letting your partner know that his or her actions or words prompted your feelings.

Frequently the anger that fuels a fight is churned up in this manner: I feel you're blaming me, so I get defensive and blame you. The battle is on.

The more highly developed the skill of talking, the easier it will be to handle anger any time of the day.

To practice communication that mixes fact with feeling, watch and then discuss a television program together. You'll likely see how two persons can view and respond to the one situation very differently. (Your discussions might even help you get to know your husband or wife as well as you know the characters on TV.) Take the time to talk about what you see, the facts of and feelings about a situation.

Similarly, talk together about the books and magazines you read. Describe what you like and what thoughts your reading provokes. You'll be sharing life—and learning to communicate in a meaningful way.

You and your partner might also investigate together the geographic area in which you live. I (Robert) used to live in Salem, Oregon, which is blessed with a great recreational river that many of the local residents had never visited. Salem is the capital city of the state, but I knew many people who had never bothered to go into the uniquely designed capitol building, although people came from other parts of the nation to go through it. Few locales are truly boring, though the people unwilling to explore the area may be. Looking together will enlarge your communication skills as you talk about what you find.

The Bible says that God "has in these last days spoken to us by His Son" (Hebrews 1:2) and "when He, the Spirit of truth, has come, He will guide you into all truth; for He will not speak on His own authority, but whatever He hears He will speak, and He will tell you things to come" (John 16:13). God expresses His love and care for us by speaking through His Word and His Spirit. If God so values communication that He speaks to us and listens when we pray, sing or praise Him, surely we should value open communication with our mates. Your thoughts are important enough to share. Express your desires, joys and feelings—not just your conclusions.

Most couples don't have a communication problem until they get married—otherwise they would never say "I do." But just a few short months into the marriage, they find themselves going, doing and functioning—but not talking to each other in a meaningful way. During courtship, couples talk about everything, trying to adjust to their lives together.

Let me warn you that if you don't keep talking about

everything, the only thing you'll have to talk about when a problem arises is the problem itself. Declaring, "We need to sit down and talk this problem out" seldom produces the intended effect unless lines of communication already exist. If a couple cannot meaningfully talk about things they agree on, how can they truly communicate in areas of disagreement?

The partners of a new marriage learn to communicate by talking. About what? Most anything. Discuss how tall a telephone pole is. How much weight does an electric wire support? Why do birds fly south in the winter? What does tapioca come from? How many reflectors are there in a mile of freeway? How much paint does it take to paint the lines on all the freeways in the state? Who cares? Nobody. But with such nonintimidating talk, you build a road of communication with your partner. When problems come, the repair trucks can travel that route. Every word is like a piece of gravel held together with asphalt or cement and paving the road of communication. If you can't converse on nonthreatening subjects, you won't talk when trouble comes; you'll argue and fight.

As we learned to talk, we can learn to express ourselves clearly. As in any other art form, practice can make one proficient, and the results are worth the practice. How do you practice clarity in your speech? Read a statement in a magazine or book, and then pause and think: How would I have said that? With today's mass communication, we too often quote someone else instead of formulating and articulating our own thoughts. How would *you* express a certain sentiment? When reading or listening to others speak, ask yourself if it could be said more artfully, directly or descriptively.

From a far hillside, an old Indian chief observed a 1940s atomic test. As he watched the great mushroom cloud ascend, he said, "Hm! I wish I'd said that!" He knew that smoke signal was out of his league.

Sometimes a speaker's vocabulary makes you feel as if his or her communication is "too big" to duplicate; yet you can learn from it. Even Scripture reading can be used to increase vocabulary skills. After reading a passage, ask yourself, How would I say that using my usual vocabulary? For instance, try to rephrase the familiar verse, "For God so loved the world that He gave His only begotten Son, that whoever believes in Him should not perish but have everlasting life" (John 3:16). Here's our attempt: "God's expression of love was Jesus Christ, and if I believe in that expression of love, He has promised me eternal life." In rephrasing the verse, we learn to communicate by vocalizing what is in our hearts.

Play with words—as you're driving down the road and reading billboards, as you hear songs on the radio. Rewrite the lines and increase your skill with words.

Initiating Communication

Years ago when my (Robert's) children were still home, my wife and I sensed a lack of communication. Since I lived in the public eye and tended to use my home as a place of escape from people, I was sometimes negligent in talking to my own family. But Shirley devised a unique way to help break down this lack of communication. She purchased and hung a dog house plaque that included a detachable papa dog, mama dog and two puppies. When a family member did something wrong or offended someone else in the family, his or her dog was moved into the dog house. To get out, that person was required to pay some sort of forfeit.

This may seem crude to you, but it was good for our family, because it "forced" me to communicate with them. Hurts weren't allowed to fester. They were out in the open for discussion. What was wrong proved to be less important than the opportunity to discuss it with the family members.

In addition to the dog-house motivation for communication, we established a "grace period." Right after dinner on Fridays, we lingered at the table and said, "There will be no punishment for anything said at this time. You can tell us anything; it is forgiven in advance." Our goal was to establish open acceptance to entice open expression in the family. I'll never forget the time our daughter waited until the Friday grace period to tell me she had dented the car fender while backing out of the garage earlier in the week. Since I had not previously noticed the dent, she wasn't punished. We kept our promise regarding our grace.

You may say, Oh, I wouldn't do that with my children! Perhaps not, though you might with someone else's. Similarly, you might not extend such grace to your own spouse, though you would to another person's. Such acceptance can seem threatening when it's so close to home. But when we're afraid to communicate, relational problems will only escalate. Destroy that fear, and talking becomes easier.

A problem's solution starts with communication, but that communication must be honest and open. Open expression demands open acceptance. Clarity of speech must be matched with clarity of hearing. This is repeatedly demonstrated in the ministry of Jesus. Knowing that the scribes and Pharisees sought to trick Him in His words, Christ carefully guarded His message, using parables and allegories. The bias of His listeners' minds made open conversation difficult if not dangerous. But to His disciples Jesus spoke plainly, as He knew their openness to listen and respond to what He said.

Communicating Compliments and Complaints

All dog trainers emphasize praising the animal for proper performance, and child experts also say that, unless we praise our children for good behavior, we have no right to punish them for bad behavior. Unfortunately, this principle is often forgotten in husband-wife relationships. Many marriages have almost gone "down the drain" simply because one partner didn't communicate positively to the other.

It seems more natural to speak of our complaints than to give a compliment. But the labor of preparing an evening meal can be quickly forgotten at the sound of "That was a good meal, darling. Thanks!" An aching back and blisters on one's palms don't hurt quite so much when a wife brags on what a good job the husband has done on a handyman's project. Honest praise and recognition are especially meaningful when they come from those closest to us.

Many women, especially those raising children and confined to the house for lengthy periods, suffer depression as a result of a poor self-image. That weak image is not necessarily connected to their physical appearance but to the lack of acceptance they feel from those around them. Husbands, your praise is important in developing and maintaining your wife's view of herself. On the job, an employer or coworkers give positive strokes. In the home, those strokes must come from the husband. Furthermore, a discontented woman can make domestic peace impossible, so self-interest as well as love should lead a husband to undergird his wife continually with expressions of appreciation and praise.

Speaking of vocalizing praise, here's a guideline for dealing with relatives and in-laws: in their presence compliment, never complain about, your mate. Belittling your husband or wife in their company is not only unkind, but it can also dig gulfs that challenge even the best bridge builder.

As we faithfully communicate praise to our mates, we earn the right to communicate about problems in the marriage as well. When you do talk about problems, remember to address the issues in terms of the emotion you're feeling because of the problem. If we can say to our mates, "I'm getting the feeling that such-and-such is true," or, "When you do that, I get such-and-such a feeling," we're talking about our feelings, not about what we've decided we have to do. When we start talking directly about the problem, we tend to suggest we've solved the problem and are expecting our spouses to conform to our conclusions, although they haven't had any input into the formation of those conclusions. But if we talk about our emotions, our mates can also talk about those emotions; we interact about why we have those emotions, and the problem can be dealt with by *both partners,* not just by one.

Of course this kind of communication takes time. Do you value your marital friendship enough to preserve it? You might take a lesson from the complaint department of a large store or, better still, a troubleshooter at a mechanic's garage. When customers come in complaining about a purchase or a repair job, it's amazing to watch those "complaint handlers" soak the emotion out of the complaint and send the people away smiling. If they care enough to do that for a customer's sake (or their employee's sake), how much more care should we exert for a marriage's sake! If some husbands treated their business customers the way they treat their wives, and if some wives treated their best friends the way they treat their husbands, they would soon have no customers or friends! We must take time to handle marital problems with care. We have vowed ourselves to that mate forever. We dare not make unnecessary waves but need to settle problems by dealing with emotions and then altering underlying situations so those emotions are not aggravated again.

Careless, cutting or cruel words have a way of destroying any further conversation. Ugly names, defamation of character and declarations of inadequacies hurled in anger stick into the soul of a person like a knife into the flesh of the body. The wounds heal slowly. We may think we were justified in saying those things (to get our point across), but we really weren't communicating at all. We were cutting, slandering and destroying someone.

To start a discussion with "I want a divorce," for example, is to slam the door on any solutions to the problem. Some claim that when we're angry we tell the real truth. We disagree. When angry we use extreme words, but those words are remembered long after the problem has been forgotten. We need to keep in mind that winning the argument is far less important than winning our mate's continued affections.

Disagreements are like taking showers in this respect: they're necessary but private. When taking a shower we shut the door, and so it should be when we deal with our problems. Don't fight with or criticize your spouse in front of others, even the children. Deal with the positive things in public and the negative things in private. Once you take care of those problems, you can come out of the private room, recognizing that problems are normal but that they must pass away.

Don't waste your time on warfare; use your time together to build your tomorrows. Build memories now. As you grow older and have less energy to fulfill dreams, those memories will become more and more important. You'll be able to look back and say, "We have done...We have been...We have seen...."

We dare not wait until the children are grown and gone from home before we start communicating. Learning the art of communication early will build fulfillment and happiness all the days of our lives.

Worksheet

Ken and Kathy are now happily married. They have made a covenant with God and each other that this marriage is "until death us do part."

One evening, Kathy came home before Ken. Because it was hot and humid, she put on a loose, light nightgown. As Kathy was cooking dinner, Ken arrived. He took one look at her and hugged her, hoping "something more" would develop.

As Ken put his arms around Kathy, she firmly stated, "Don't touch me. It's too hot!"

What was Kathy and Ken's communication problem? What did Kathy say in nonverbal actions?

If you were Ken, how would you communicate with Kathy?

Communication frequently falters because two people have differing basic concepts and expectations of their relationship and each other. In the following pages is a true/false questionnaire. Make a copy for each partner. Working alone, fill out the questionnaire, and then compare your answers to your mate's. Discuss your beliefs as an exercise in communication.

What I Believe

True or False (circle one)

T   F   1. Avoid problems; they will disappear in time.

T   F   2. Being assertive means never giving in to the other person's wishes.

T   F   3. If I express my feelings, I'll lose control.

T   F   4. It's best to avoid issues that bring up conflict.

T   F   5. Christians have fewer problems than nonbelievers.

T   F   6. I have to take responsibility for others.

T   F   7. A situation is always black or white; to have gray is confusion.

T   F   8. Men are by nature insensitive and self-centered.

T   F   9. The less I disclose about myself, the better off I will be.

T   F   10. If the man is in a good place spiritually, the family is automatically there.

T   F   11. If a woman pushes a man's red button, it's OK for him to hit her.

T   F   12. If a woman sees a man cry, she loses all respect for him.

T   F   13. It's OK for a man to fight physically, but not a woman.

T   F   14. Men are more logical than women.

T   F   15. A man must not be vulnerable or lose control.

T   F   16. Men are superior to women.

T   F   17. Whatever I do, it must be done perfectly.

T   F   18. We can control life by controlling our thoughts.

T   F   19. I am responsible for the happiness of others.

T   F   20. Education and training are more important for men than for women.

FOUR

THE EAST
FOUNDATION

Are Your Spiritual
Concepts Compatible?

"Who are you, Lord?"
—Acts 9:5

Some years ago, a fine Christian woman introduced me (Robert) to her fiancé and wanted to talk about their impending marriage. To my surprise, in our discussion David said, "I'm a Jew. I attend the synagogue."

Betty turned to me and said, "Pastor, will this make any difference in our marriage?"

Looking her squarely in the eyes, I said, "Betty, what does the name of Jesus Christ mean to you?"

She quickly responded, "Well, He's God's Son and my Savior."

Turning to the young man, I asked, "What does the name of Jesus Christ mean to you?"

Without hesitancy he said, "I hate to say it, but to me He's an imposter, an anti-God, a false claimer."

Addressing both of them I said, "Will this make any difference?"

They left my study but for some time stood talking outside my study window. Eventually he got into his car, and she got into hers, but then they both got out and talked again for half an hour. I could see her shaking her head, and they returned to their separate cars and drove away. Betty eventually called off their wedding plans, as she wasn't willing to start building a marriage without a shared spiritual foundation. Several years later, it was my joy to unite Betty in marriage with a fine Christian man, to whom she is still happily married.

Joining together in a common commitment to the Lord Jesus Christ makes all the difference for a marriage.

It's a fundamental law of life: "For as he thinks in his heart, so is he" (Proverbs 23:7). Think of the advertising world, constantly bombarding us with thought-altering messages. Executives know that if they can change our minds we will purchase their products. Politicians spend vast sums of money to influence our opinions before a major election; they know that our thoughts will govern our behavior at the polls.

Our concepts—what we think about people, situations or things—form our philosophy of life and alter our approach to living. Even if much of what you read in this book slips from your memory, remember this simple sentence: *your relationship with God depends upon your concept of God.* Proper spiritual relationships depend upon proper spiritual concepts. As we think, we will be and behave. This means that compatible spiritual concepts are important to a marriage. Without them, the spiritual foundation will be split instead of firm.

Though our concepts of God don't change His nature,

they can limit our approach to Him and His intervention in our lives. "What you see is what you get" applies to far more than certain computer software. What we see in God is all we can appropriate of God.

We form concepts long before we recognize them as such. They come from at least four sources: observation, information, evaluation and application.

Our first source of understanding is our *observation*. Before we ever understood word patterns, we began to form concepts by observing life around us. We learned to recognize our parents and draw conclusions about them. As long as our eyesight remains, we will have this source of information-gathering. And the more we observe, the broader our expanse of knowledge.

Let's say you took a pair of binoculars and looked across a park. You might see a couple talking, seated on a bench. By reducing the power setting and broadening the scope of vision, you might see that the bench is under a tree. With further adjustment of the magnification, you might observe that they're alongside a lake and watching a swan swimming toward them. The more you're able to observe, the more complete your concept of this couple.

So it is with spiritual concepts. The more we observe Jesus and the things of God, the broader our spiritual concepts will be, and the stronger our Christian life will become.

But not all concepts come from personal observation. Many are formed on the basis of *information* given to us by others. We develop our spiritual concepts from information passed on by our parents and Sunday school teachers, through our schools and various organizations we join, from acquaintances and spiritual leaders. The more faith we have in the source, the deeper the belief. Dad said it, so it's inviolate to us. The absoluteness of parental authority creates concepts that children will have to deal with for the rest of their lives.

More than likely your concepts of marriage originated in your childhood home. Did anyone take you aside and teach you how to be a husband or a wife? Probably not. We enter into marriage thinking that our parents' relationship is what it's all about. Occasionally, a childhood home stands as a powerful example of what marriage should *not* be. Even then, however, it influences one's concepts about married life.

A third formative source of concepts is *evaluation*. As we mature, we examine and evaluate what was previously given as authoritative information. This process often begins in high school and is amplified during the college years, when we're bombarded with so many conflicting philosophies. We are forced to evaluate what we have firmly believed in light of new concepts presented to us. Our personal judgment now influences the formation of our concepts, including our spiritual ones. Those fortunate enough to grow up in Christian homes first accepted the spiritual concepts of their parents without question. As they matured, they had to judge those concepts and initiate their own personal relationship with Jesus Christ.

The fourth step in forming a concept is *application*. After we have examined and evaluated observations we've made and information we've been given, we must put them into action to see if they work in our lives. At this point, our concepts become foundations.

It's unlikely that any concept we embrace is perfect or complete. As we mature, our concepts need to mature. As truth is progressively unveiled, we need to make room for progressive development in our concepts, both natural and spiritual. For instance, when a child asks, "Mommy, where did I come from?" the answer, "You came out of Mommy's tummy" is both honest and satisfactory. But there's something wrong if that child, grown to age twenty-four, has not increased in understanding of childbirth. Though new information would not contradict the initial concept, it would enlighten, broaden and make it more meaningful.

Likewise, many of our concepts of God need to be enlightened with fresh input, not erasing the old but augmenting it. We don't deny the beginning to reach toward the end; we expand and extend the original concept into a more mature expression of life. The Bible says, "But grow in the grace and knowledge of our Lord and Savior Jesus Christ" (2 Peter 3:18). Spiritual concepts grow with input and ripen with age.

Why is this enlargement of our spiritual concepts so vital? Because our relationship with God depends on our concept of God. If we view Him as One who is angry, vengeful and wrathful, our relationship with Him will be fearful. If we conceive a passive God who is all love, our relationship with Him may be careless, as we may fail to recognize a God who is just and who brings judgment upon those who disobey Him.

Just how do you picture God? Is He a divine Santa Claus seated in the heavens, waiting for a special day to distribute gifts? Is He instead reticent to give anything, requiring us to beg, plead and threaten for everything we get from Him? (Unfortunately, this second view is the prevailing heathen concept.)

Again, God is not formed in our concepts. He has always been, and everything we see on this earth and in the universe beyond us has been created by His expressed will. The book of Isaiah repeatedly quotes God as saying, "I am the Lord, and there is no other; there is no God besides Me" (Isaiah 45:5). Despite the nearly fanatical belief of multiple thousands of people, there is not a Muslim Allah; he doesn't even exist. Baal never was born, and Confucius is a code of ethics. The Jehovah-God, the "I AM THAT I AM," is the one true God. There isn't a Catholic God, a

Protestant God or a Jewish God. Even within the evangelical world, there isn't a Baptist God, a Methodist God or a Pentecostal God; there is one God. Our differences are in our conceptual views of that God and how He should be approached.

We all need continual enlargement of our spiritual concepts. This can come through a regular pattern of Bible study—not because we want to "be right," but because we need to have a right concept of God, who has revealed Himself in His Word.

Commonality of Christian Concepts

Paul the apostle wrote, "There is one body and one Spirit, just as you were called in one hope of your calling; one Lord, one faith, one baptism; one God and Father of all, who is above all, and through all, and in you all" (Ephesians 4:4-6). Seeing many churches in one town or hearing many doctrines preached makes it difficult for some to believe that there is far more unity than disunity among the Protestant churches. Though our common denominator is the Lord Jesus Christ, we all tend to be nearsighted. We fail to reach for the greater concept of God.

Because our understanding of Christ and of God generally is limited, our teaching to others is less than complete. Baptists focus on the security found in Christ Jesus. Nazarenes focus on Christ's great work of sanctification. Pentecostals tend to focus on the gifts and graces of the Holy Spirit in Christ Jesus. Each emphasizes one concept of God, magnifying that truth in precept and practice. Those views, however, are complementary, not contradictory. If we would blend the elements into one concept (rather than blame the other parties for lacking the concept we hold so sacred), we would more clearly see the large measure of our living God.

It isn't necessary for all Christians to agree on every point of doctrine, however, and neither is it necessary for the two partners in a marriage to be united on every point. Because our views of God are so personal, we doubt you would find two people in the world who agreed completely. There's really a lot of leeway for differences of opinion. Lack of unity on the basics, however, will spell disaster for the marriage, as the main weight-bearing wall of the house will sink and subject the whole house to destruction.

We've heard it argued that people honestly and earnestly working together can overcome vast differences in fundamental spiritual concepts. But it's like trying to add three-fourths and one-half. It can't be done unless one fraction is changed, allowing for a common denominator. When the one-half is changed to two-fourths, the two can be brought together.

The common denominator essential for a spiritually strong marriage is a belief that Jesus Christ is God's Son, sent into this world as the only Savior, and that all need to trust in Him as personal Savior. This foundational common denominator of faith in Christ Jesus will support the marriage. Basic beliefs have nothing to do with water baptism, speaking in tongues or other doctrinal issues. Those "numbers" above the line don't have to be identical as long as a husband and wife share a common denominator below the fraction line. You may be as different as one-fourth and five-hundred-eighty-eight-fourths, but you can still work together on the same foundation: Jesus Christ, God's Son, your Savior.

This is not open to argument: "For no other foundation can anyone lay than that which is laid, which is Jesus Christ" (1 Corinthians 3:11). Upon this common denominator we build our relationships—first with God, then with each other.

Conflict or Concord in Christian Concepts

"Do not be unequally yoked together with unbelievers. For what fellowship has righteousness with lawlessness? And what communion has light with darkness? And what accord has Christ with Belial? Or what part has a believer with an unbeliever?" (2 Corinthians 6:14-15). This is a New Testament commandment written to ensure the joys of marriage, not to limit them. God isn't trying to prevent marriage; He is endeavoring to prevent misery. God our Creator understands the issues far better than we do. Many marriages have failed because couples have attempted to build a home without the firm foundation of common spiritual concepts and commitment.

Any couple planning to marry with unequal spiritual concepts should reevaluate whether they are willing to build a marriage without a spiritual foundation. We are clearly assured, "Whoever calls on the name of the Lord shall be saved" (Acts 2:21), and the days of preparation for marriage would be a wonderful time for both parties to commit their lives to the Lord Jesus Christ and acknowledge Him as Lord and Savior. A spiritual foundation is born of the Spirit of God by faith in Jesus Christ, and then it is developed by the couple together.

Since the Scriptures prohibit unequal spiritual yoking, equal yoking must be possible. This doesn't require equality in experience (one party might be a Bible school graduate and the other a new Christian) but an equal commitment to Christ, which will continue to mature as our knowledge of God increases.

Different people have different concepts of us (Robert and Judson), depending on the role in which they see us: pastor, teacher, husband, father, grandfather, son, brother, friend, neighbor, customer, employer and employee.

Similarly, we see God in many different ways, though He

is one God. As a Christian couple, see how many ways you view God similarly. Validate (or discard) concepts according to God's book as new light and revelation are given.

Constructing Christian Concepts

The spiritual foundation of your marriage can be regularly strengthened as you increase your common understanding of God and His ways. Far too many people know a lot about God without actually knowing God Himself. The more we study about God in the Bible, the better we know Him. It is a joy to see young couples studying the Word together long before marriage. Many agree on a portion of Scripture to be read privately. Then they discuss it as a scheduled part of their date.

"But," you say, "we don't go out on a date for spiritual reasons." Wouldn't it be worthwhile to consider doing so? Our playboy-oriented society has set a norm: be attracted physically, then develop a relationship. The Bible teaches the exact opposite: be attracted to a person because of that individual's worth and to explore the possibility of a life together and let the physical relationship grow out of that higher relationship. Because we are one-third spirit, we need to develop that area of being together.

As Christian counselors and ministers of the gospel, we'd like to offer a few nuggets of advice to help any couple develop the spirituality of their marriage. Read and discuss the Word, before and after your marriage. You may both be Christians, but that doesn't automatically mean you have a Christian home. A Christian home isn't two Christians living in the same house; it's a home that establishes Jesus Christ as its foundation stone. Its members make provision for praise, worship, service, tithing, ministry and Bible study. When the husband takes his place as head of the home in spiritual matters, the priorities of the home seem to fall into a proper sequence.

The Bible teaches that when two people get married they become one. Heaven isn't full of computers, but we like to think that, on a wedding day, heaven's computer copies two separate files and combines them into one. The "Bill" file combined with the "Mary" file become the "Bary" file. There's still a file for each person, but this new file records their combined lives; spiritual input is made jointly as well as individually.

Early in marriage, one partner may have more spiritual knowledge than the other. If the wife knows more of the Bible than the husband, she should share that knowledge. The husband is called to control his pride and learn what she is sharing with him. Similarly, the husband needs to share his knowledge of spiritual truths with his wife, and she should learn from him.

Before the wedding vows, *introduce prayer into your relationship* and carry it into your marriage. Don't wait for the children to come before establishing a family altar. Let it anticipate their coming. Even the simplest prayer can enlarge your spiritual concepts; thanking and praising God together will strengthen your faith. It might surprise you to know that surveys indicate that fewer than 50 percent of evangelical Christians take time to ask God's blessing over their meals. They don't know what a beautiful spiritual bond they're missing as a family. Mealtime grace lays the foundation for further expressions of thanks to God. Doesn't the Bible say, "Giving thanks always for all things to God the Father in the name of our Lord Jesus Christ" (Ephesians 5:20)? Wouldn't it be wonderful to get up in the morning and say, "Thank You, God, for a night of rest" and have your wife or husband agree with you?

Even before marriage, it's good to discuss how much of your individual and collective lives you will give to the Lord's ministry. Will you attend Sunday services together?

How about prayer meetings? Will you sing in the choir or continue to usher? Marriage should never be a replacement for Christian service but an amplification of it. Marriage will change your social life, but it needn't change your dedication to service in the church.

Complying With Christian Concepts

The Bible gives us standards and guidelines for implementing our Christian concepts in the framework of marriage. For instance, the Scriptures clearly teach that if we cannot be spiritual leaders in our homes we should not be chosen as spiritual leaders in the church of Jesus Christ.

While teaching husbands their responsibility to obey God, the Bible instructs wives to be in subjection to their husbands. It is easier to surrender your will to a person who has yielded his will to almighty God. We recommend that as part of the wedding ceremony the bride say to her bridegroom, "I love you, and I will follow you as you follow God." The husband's responsibility is to train his family and himself in the Word and ways of God. This should never be left up to the wife; she can supplement his teaching, but she cannot substitute for it.

A couple's spiritual life does not automatically enlarge or strengthen itself. It needs direction and attention, and their spiritual life touches all the other areas of married life. Because every facet of life is altered by our spiritual concept of God, because our very relationship with God Himself is dependent on our concept of God, our relationship to Him should be the number one priority, higher even than our marriages. This is not to suggest that our marriages and our commitments to Christ should be competitive; the two should be harmonious. Indeed, if husband and wife share a basic commitment to the Lord, their growth in Him will only strengthen their marriage.

Worksheet

Ken and Kathy have a problem! Ken has been doing well at work, so well that his company wants to promote him, but that would mean he'd have to work on Sundays and Wednesday evenings (church time).

Ken wants the promotion and knows that, if he doesn't take it now, he'll never have the chance again. Though Kathy wants Ken to succeed in his career, she is concerned that he will stop seeking God.

Is Ken compromising by accepting the promotion?

Ken and Kathy need to talk honestly with each other about every feeling and thought regarding the ramifications of all possible decisions. They also need to seek God in prayer for His wisdom and revelation.

FIVE

THE SOUTH FOUNDATION

Have You Considered Your Family Backgrounds?

"...God, whom I serve...
as my forefathers did. "
—2 Timothy 1:3

For generations, one Indian tribe that lived in the mountains had worshipped the great salmon that swam in the river far below them. A second tribe lived in the valley and worshipped the magnificent elk that roamed the high mountains. Salmon was staple food of the valley people, while the mountain people freely ate the elk so revered by the valley people.

One day a mountain brave came down and met a fair valley maiden who was gathering wildflowers at the base of the mountain. Their eyes met; their hearts melted. Although it proved complicated, they arranged an inter-tribal marriage and prepared to live happily ever after.

Everything went fine—until she went to prepare their first meal together. She was horrified to discover that he wanted to eat her god, and he was shocked to discover that she was cooking his god.

"I'm marrying you, not your family!" It's a common courtship assertion. But no matter how determined one may be, family background plays a large role in the marital relationship. Each person is a product of environmental and family backgrounds, a product of a society that he or she did not create. We can't alter our roots. We can't change our parentage or the family society in which we were born and raised. It's useless to say, "I don't want to be who I am."

Physically, we are what we are by genetic selection, and often we don't like it. Tall people often wish they were shorter, and most short people wish to be tall. The Bible asks rhetorically, "Which of you by worrying can add one cubit to his stature?" (Luke 12:25). (However, we can—and do—add to our horizontal measurement!) Like you, I (Robert) am what I am in spite of what I wish I were. I am six feet, two inches tall because my dad was six feet, one-and-a-half inches tall, and my grandfather was taller than that. I have blue eyes because my mother had blue eyes. I am the result of my ancestral genes, and the more quickly I accept that, the more rapidly I can adjust to it.

Everything we do is affected by the combination of our genetic background, family background, culture and training. Our customs and habit patterns have been ingrained in us from before birth. It doesn't matter whether we're Hispanic, German, Italian or English; each group of people has its own inherited and cultural characteristics that can be viewed positively or negatively. Some people say that Germans are stubborn, but the Germans identify this trait as determination. Many Americans think the English lack a sense of humor, while the English feel their humor is highly refined. In entering a marriage relationship, each partner has certain characteristics that can either enhance or hinder the relationship.

Family and individual characteristics will manifest themselves in subtle ways. Have you ever noticed a developer building a block of identical houses? Then the block houses are sold to persons with different family backgrounds, and in a short time each house looks noticeably different from all the others. The personality of the owner shows through. There's no covering it up.

My Way Is Not Your Way

God seems to rejoice in the infinite variety in human cultures. But the differences can create problems in marriage. Love often starts out blind. A person from one society meets a person from another, and emotion bursts onto the scene: "You must be mine for the rest of our days." The depth of this emotion often overwhelms sound reasoning. Then, sometime after the honeymoon, the emotion begins to wane. The two backgrounds collide, as in the tale of the two young Indians.

The further apart two people's backgrounds are, the more potential for conflict. For example, suppose people of two races marry. Their differences in facial features or skin pigmentation may not cause problems, but differences between their two cultures may create monumental headaches.

Cultures do make a difference. One culture may be lenient in its treatment of misbehaving children, while another enforces strict discipline. In one culture, husbands may make all important decisions, while in another wives expect to participate equally. When people from these cultures marry, the potential for serious conflict is enormous.

Even trivial differences can be annoying. My (Robert's) wife's family name is Johnson, and the Johnsons had a dining habit that my sister-in-law continues. For lunch they often ate sandwiches, but they were never made in the kitchen. A choice of ingredients was placed on the table, and each person made his or her own sandwich. What's wrong with that? you ask. Absolutely nothing, but I don't enjoy it. In our family, the sandwiches were made in the kitchen. The multiple-choice approach says to me, "Wait a minute—that's a Johnson way, not a Cornwall way." I've been married for more than forty years, and these different patterns still churn up an emotional response in me.

Whether you realize it or not, your habits can be far removed from those of even your sweetheart who grew up next door to you and whose national heritage you share. In marriage, you may try to bring those two worlds together, only to learn that what you did in your world clashes with what your spouse has always done—not because one is wrong and the other is right, but because the two are different.

Think about the way you butter your bread. Do you take a slice of butter off the butter dish and smear it across the bread, or do you use the butter knife to put a pat of butter on your bread plate, return the butter knife to the dish, break the slice of bread neatly in half and butter each portion as you eat it?

You may ask, What difference does it make? None—none at all. But families who learn to do it one way can look at the person who does it another way as being crude or rude.

Obviously, those are just little differences around the dinner table. But stop and think. You're going to live with the person you marry twenty-four hours a day. You'll live in the same house, sleep in the same bed, use the same bathroom, eat with the same silverware and hang your clothes in the same closet. So often the "cute little ways" enjoyed during courtship become irritants when repeated endlessly in marriage, and habit patterns unseen before marriage can fuel serious disagreements after.

The proverbial joke about a couple fighting over how to squeeze toothpaste from a tube is really no joke at all. It happens—all too often.

The early conflicts in a marriage usually stem from these familial differences. Disagreements may erupt over inconsequential issues, such as the way one dresses or holds the fork at dinner. But they *will* erupt if two people view their own way as right and the other person's as wrong.

One Foundation Affects the Others

There's no escaping these differences in family background, and they will deeply affect all the other foundations of marriage. Look at communication. A person from a family where members yell and gesture to make a point will communicate that way in marriage. Coming from a family that harbors grudges, keeps secrets or pouts instead of talks, a person will do the same with a spouse.

Family background obviously affects our spiritual concepts. So much of what we do and think in regard to God and the church is learned from others. The same God who sees us in our "Sunday best" also sees us in our birthday suits, for He is everywhere present. He's not impressed by how we dress when we go to church, yet we dress up for the occasion as a result of our backgrounds. Devotional habits, worship patterns, church attendance and concepts of faith were likely formed in the family unit.

In similar manner, the sexual concepts we bring into marriage are based almost entirely on our family backgrounds. Did our parents hug and kiss a lot? Did our families rarely express affection? Some persons have never seen their parents embrace. Others as a matter of course may have seen "too much" in their parents' bedroom. Even the way we learned about sex can affect our attitude toward it. Was sex a forbidden subject in the home, or was it an open topic for discussion? Were we taught about sexuality, or did we "discover" it from listening to others? All these factors will influence our sexual relationship in marriage.

The foundation of finances will also be affected by our family backgrounds. Although money is often a problem area in marriage, the actual abundance or lack of money seldom creates the problem. Conflicts arise from the way money is *handled*, and money management is learned in one's youth.

Some families are very careful about their spending. They don't make a purchase until they have money available to pay for it. Other families use their credit cards to the limit. They're constantly paying for past purchases. One family may settle for fewer material goods so they can have a bank reserve. Another family spends every cent earned on cars, furniture, clothes and recreation. In marriage, both of those backgrounds often come together. The ensuing fireworks are inevitable.

As distasteful as it is to mention divorce in a book written for people about to get married, it's important to note that family background and attitude toward divorce may well influence the stability of the new marriage. A person from a broken home may have one primary model for resolving marital problems: quitting the marriage.

Some of these insights may be alarming, but simply recognizing that many of the tensions in a marriage come from diverse family backgrounds allows us to move ahead and work to overcome them.

Blending Backgrounds

Marriage is far more than an emotional feeling or mere sexual gratification. Marriage is two people living together in covenant for the rest of their natural lives. God's design for this covenant wasn't life-long conflict. What's the alternative? Adapting—blending two family backgrounds into a new, revised life-style that chooses the best from two worlds and seasons the mix with unique, original ideas.

In the emotional ecstasy of young love, it's difficult to see how much energy the blending of two family cultures can require. It takes work, but it can be done.

The first step to avoiding conflict over familial differences is to recognize they exist. Then there's no need to declare war over them.

Many familial differences can be adjusted to before marriage. Spend time observing the family of your prospective husband or wife. One of the values of a long engagement is having time to determine if your two families will mix well.

How do they do things? What are their speech patterns? Are they serious, playful, given to teasing or withdrawn? You will be living the rest of your life with those traits. What is your future in-laws' philosophy of life? How do they handle money, raise their children, treat the things of God? What is their stance toward education? Is college or finishing high school important to them? What roles do the wife and husband play? How do they relate to each other? These points, as well as others, need to be discussed openly and honestly. Where do you stand in terms of differing ideas and habits?

Even before marriage, discuss each other's bedroom and bathroom habits. How compatible are the two of you in the way you prepare for bed? Do you take your clothes off and drop them on the floor where they stay for a week—or until

Mother comes and picks them up? Or do you put the dirty clothes into the hamper? Do you hang up your suit coats every night or let them collect on the back of a chair? Do you sleep with the window open or closed? Where do you put the wet bath towels?

Recognizing and even discussing differences won't bring peace to a household. Peace comes as two people acknowledge "your way" and "my way" and work to establish a third "our way." The sooner the first two can blend into the third, the smoother living together will be. For this process to proceed, however, both people have to let go of "my way" as the one and only right way. Put on this attitude: "I will not defend myself; I will evaluate other ways of doing things and discuss them with my partner."

One of the early joys in marriage is comparing how you do something and how your partner does it, or how you think differently about any given subject. Instead of each of you trying to prove yourself right, together try to create a third way of doing or saying something that's better than either one of your original ways.

Let's try an experiment. Fold your hands. Now look at your hands. Is your right thumb over your left thumb, or your left over your right? Unclasp your hands, and fold them a second time, this time deliberately reversing the placement of your thumbs. Your fingers just don't seem to mesh, do they? They feel strange, fat and clumsy. Try this experiment in a roomful of people and you'll see that there is no right or wrong way to fold hands. By nature, some do it one way and some the other.

It will be this way with many things in the marriage. One way of "folding" may seem comfortable to one partner but irritating to the other. Adjusting to do it in a new way may feel awkward, but no one needs to know how strange it feels—unless you insist upon telling them.

Arguments in a marriage seldom involve issues that are

morally right or wrong. Most verbal disagreements ultimately involve a defense of a family heritage. Having been taught by the authoritative family that this is an acceptable way (maybe even the "right" way) of doing something, we contend that it must be done that way here and now and forever more. If our way is unacceptable to our mate, we get defensive, and an argument ensues. If these family backgrounds are to be successfully combined, we must first recognize the differences for what they are—differences— and then stop asserting one way as vastly superior over another way.

Sometimes the best way to conquer is to compromise. There's nothing wrong with compromise when it pertains to marital adjustment; it's the basis for practical living, and it's certainly wiser than war. In the little irritants or differences of opinion, (1) consider, (2) compromise and (3) become compatible. All the while, realize that character traits adversely affecting the marriage need to be brought into conformity to the will of God. A person's character can grow more Christlike by faith in Christ. Your compromise can become easier as your spirit draws nearer to God.

Backgrounds Can Be Converted

Couples whose spiritual foundation is firm are blessed with hope, even when they're from divergent backgrounds. God's Word assures us, "Therefore, if anyone is in Christ, he is a new creation; old things have passed away; behold, all things have become new" (2 Corinthians 5:17). One translation puts it, "...the old life has passed away; behold the new life has come." Christians cannot excuse their own irritating behavior or warped character by saying, "I'm English (or Dutch, German, black or white), and that's just the way my people are!" It's wrong to give place to besetting sins or arrogant attitudes because of our heritage; when we surrendered our lives to Christ Jesus, we entered into a new heritage. God became our Father, and His Holy Spirit with us is now working to produce the character of God in us.

Since Christ's Spirit is resident in believers, in a Christian marriage both parties should display the fruit of the Spirit rather than the fruit of their past family heritages. Paul tells us that "the fruit of the Spirit is love, joy, peace, longsuffering, kindness, goodness, faithfulness, gentleness, self-control" (Galatians 5:22-23). Though those virtues may not have been evident in our childhood homes, we have a spiritual parentage now, and regardless of our ancestral line or home life, God's Spirit becomes the nature of our changed lives.

There's nothing automatic about this, however. It requires our cooperation; it's a matter of choice. We can choose the heritage of our earthly father or the new heritage offered by our heavenly Father.

Just imagine what can happen in a home where both the husband and wife dare to say, "We give the present to Him to be altered. We consign our future into the hands of God so He can shape us into the image of Jesus Christ—so that what He was, we can become." We can—and must—do this.

The old tendencies and family heritages will remain in our memory circuits, but, with God's help, we can choose to live above them. The Bible asks, "Shall we continue in sin [or the sin nature] that grace may abound? Certainly not! How shall we who died to sin live any longer in it?... Do not present your members as instruments of unrighteousness to sin, but present yourselves to God as being alive from the dead, and your members as instruments of righteousness to God.... Do you not know that to whom you present yourselves slaves to obey, you are that one's slaves whom you obey, whether of sin [leading] to death, or of obedience [leading] to righteousness?" (Romans 6:1-2,13,16).

Paul clearly says that our wills dominate our native appetites. The new creation dominates the old nature. Our willingness to conform to the image of Jesus Christ and the enabling of the Holy Spirit supersede the natural-heritage factor. Though our fundamental nature was formed long before marriage, we can be changed if we will to be different. The New Testament is full of examples of radical change. Consider Paul the zealot—changed from a persecutor of saints to a preacher of righteousness. God, who is in the business of change, always changes us for the better. Any area of our married lives that is surrendered to His control will be improved.

Worksheet

Ken and Kathy are planning their vacation, but they're at a standstill.

Kathy's idea of a vacation is to go to New York to shop and enjoy the theater as her parents always did.

Ken, on the other hand, wants to go to the mountains and stay in a log cabin. He wants to fish, hunt and hike, as he did on childhood vacations.

How can Ken and Kathy compromise so they both enjoy *their* vacation, not just his or hers?

SIX

THE WEST
FOUNDATION

What About
Sexual Compatibility?

"Marriage is honorable among all,
and the bed undefiled."
—Hebrews 13:4

s natural as sex is, sexual compatibility between husbands and wives is far from automatic. Even when they genuinely love each other, serious problems can exist. Consider the situation of the husband who wrote the following:

"My wife and I need help. I feel that all our troubles stem from one cause. My wife does not want to have intercourse with me, and I cannot accept this. The situation has existed all of our eighteen years of marriage. We currently have relationships about once a month. This occurs normally after many days of my frustrating attempts to have her respond. Then it is not a loving affair, but a surrender or duty attitude on her part. I love my wife. She is an outstanding wife, mother and friend. Except that she does not physically love me. I'm afraid to face up to the fact that maybe my wife just doesn't love *me* and cannot respond to *me*. I have asked myself many times, What are you still married for? I have no answer. I don't know what to do.''*

In human beings, sexuality is biological, psychological and physiological. The presence of the sexual drive is not abnormal; its absence is. Most couples pursuing marriage worry more about sexual activity than they need to. For two healthy, normal human beings, the sexual relationship is a natural attraction. As the letter just quoted shows, however, when that relationship is not working to both partners' satisfaction, it can be a source of great frustration and pain. Our purpose in this chapter is to give a basic understanding and to anticipate some of the common causes of difficulty.

What we need as married couples is sexual compatibility, not merely sex. The amazing, recent success of organ transplants has given our generation a keen understanding of the word *compatibility*. To transplant a heart, kidney, liver or lung into a patient, multiple tests are made to determine physical compatibility between the donor and the recipient. The body will reject a transplanted organ that is not chemically or genetically compatible.

That's what we mean by sexual compatibility. Will it "take" or be "rejected"? Every man does not have a desire for every woman, or every woman for every man. In ways we don't understand completely, certain persons are attracted to particular types of people. Someone may declare, "I just love blue eyes...or red hair...or slender figures." But beyond that the person may not understand the physical

---

* Ed Wheat, *Love Life for Every Married Couple* (Grand Rapids, Mich.: Zondervan, 1980), p. 78.

and emotional attraction he or she feels for a particular woman or man.

Compatibility has nothing to do with being similar in physical build. It does not necessarily mean that two people are mentally alike, as it is not unusual to see a highly educated person married to a person with little formal education. Compatibility is not even a matter of interests and activities, for opposites tend to attract in marriage, something like opposite poles of a magnet.

Sexual compatibility seems to be a matter of the mental images the two partners have formed about sex. Sexuality is stimulated, simulated and satiated in the mind. Sexual compatibility occurs when the fact of the act satisfies the fantasy of the mind. If it satisfies the mind, it will satisfy the body. But if the mind is left unexhilarated—unfulfilled—sex is disappointing. *Dear Abby* has said that, when there are rocks in a marriage, the rocks are usually in the mattress. I wouldn't have said it that way, but she might be right.

The Fact of Sex

Though sexual compatibility is far more than sex, it cannot be divorced from sex, which is a natural physical relationship between a male and a female. Without the joining of the two reproductive systems, there can be no reproduction. For men and women, sex can also bring contentment, sharing and complementary growth and development.

The human body has natural sexual needs. God made these bodies and created the sexual drive, His method of making certain we repopulate the earth. The sexual union of husband and wife has His complete blessing.

When Noah left the ark after the flood, God said to him and his family, "Be fruitful and multiply on the earth"

(Genesis 9:1). In simple terms, God was saying, "Be sexy! Perform the sexual act."

As previously pointed out, after creating Adam, God declared, "It is not good that man should be alone; I will make him a helper comparable to him" (Genesis 2:18). Putting Adam to sleep, God borrowed one of man's ribs and fashioned from it a woman—amazing creativity. We like to believe that, when Adam awoke from his sleep and he and Eve first saw each other, they both said, "*Wow! Isn't that great!*" They desired each other sexually—*and God was present.*

In designing the sex act, it seems that God demonstrated a sense of humor. Involving the most delicate parts of our bodies, the sexual embrace almost requires the skill of a gymnast. To an observing fly on the wall, the act of lovemaking must be quite comical. Does God laugh at us from time to time?

God's design for human sexuality does not include the ability to be in the sexual act at all times. He chose to restrict intercourse to times of stimulation, giving men and women the power to arouse each other's mental desire rather than to restrict us to biological cycles over which we have little or no control, as is the case with the animals.

God made sex for pleasure and procreation, but He also made it pure. Unfortunately, Satan revels in stealing the purity of the sexual relationship. The permissive attitude of today's world, the "playboy philosophy," has overemphasized the pleasure of sex while denying the purity of sexual contact. The world says, "Anything is acceptable between consenting adults; where a willing partner cannot be found, masturbation or bestiality is acceptable. If it feels good, do it!"

If all a person wants is sex, and the person isn't concerned about offending God, perhaps marriage seems too great a price to pay for it. Sex can be had easily nowadays (the danger of venereal diseases and AIDS notwithstanding), whereas marriage is the commitment of your entire life.

The Pact of Sex

Almost any counselor who deals with human sexuality will testify, however, that the only fulfilling sexual relationships are those between a man and a woman who are pledged to each other in a covenantal relationship. They have vowed their love to each other and declared, "You are mine, and I am yours."

Marital sex is far more than safe sex; it is satisfying sex. Only in the security of the marriage vows can the imaginations of the husband and wife be fully gratified with a freedom of expression that is not laden with fear or guilt, which destroys the best of pleasure.

Consider the boy who steals a watermelon from the neighbor's field. How he anticipates the enjoyment of eating that melon! But in reality he has to eat it hiding in a dark, smelly barn; then he must cover up the evidence. In contrast, melon served at a picnic tastes far better, and the sweet aftertaste lasts longer.

In the course of a lifetime, you may encounter a number of persons with whom you might have formed a happy marriage. Once you marry, however, all options are gone. Automobiles may be changed periodically, but marriage partners should not be.

As pastors we have been told often, "I didn't make the right choice in my marriage."

We've learned to be comfortable in responding, "There is not a single 'right' choice. God lets us make our choice, and then we live to make that choice right." Marriage is a commitment to learn to live together. After a decision has been made and a pact of marriage has been entered into, it becomes a lifetime uniting of two persons. No one said marriage would always be easy or pleasant, but the joy and unifying factor of the sexual union can help to smooth over the difficult times.

The sexual fidelity of the marriage covenant needs to be protected at all times—even before you enter into it. The person you are about to marry will not benefit from hearing about every sordid part of your past. What transpired before each of you began walking into this covenantal relationship should not be discussed in detail. Sitting down to lay out all the mistakes made in the past, whether physical, mental, spiritual or sexual, is not required. Once the covenant is sealed, you have a responsibility to each other, but all (known or unknown) acts that transpired before that covenant agreement should be forgiven and forgotten. As you work on the present and your future together, accept each other at face value, and let the past be past.

The sexual foundation to marriage is not independent of the other foundations, as one side of a foundation offers strength to the others according to the stress load upon the house at any given moment. If you're at war over sexual activity, your *communication* will suffer. As for *spiritual compatibility,* you cannot have a sound relationship with God if you can't maintain a good relationship with your husband or wife. The Bible declares that strife between a husband and a wife hinders their prayers: "You husbands, dwell with them [wives] with understanding, giving honor to the wife, as to the weaker vessel, and as being heirs together of the grace of life, that your prayers may not be hindered" (1 Peter 3:7).

The foundation of *family heritage* will either be weakened or strengthened by your sexual relationship. Good sex can help override problems prompted by differences in heritage, and proper sex can set a pleasant tone in the home that will give your children a healthy heritage. Even tension caused by financial pressures can be lessened if the marriage has achieved sexual compatibility.

Though the world talks too much about sex, and in terms as low and filthy as a sewer, the church needs to talk more openly and plainly about sex and sexuality. We need to proclaim sexual compatibility as God's gift and declare openly that sex in marriage is guiltless. It needs to be divested of all the shame, fears and guilt that have been fostered upon us from our Victorian past.

The Bible says that the marriage bed is undefiled (see Hebrews 13:4). This is not to say it is undefilable. The dignity of neither partner should be compromised for the lustful pleasure of the other.

The New Testament further teaches that a husband and wife should not refrain from sexual relationship. Why tempt a spouse to turn to some other means of gratification (see 1 Corinthians 7)?

We have occasionally observed couples getting married and then rarely coming to church for the first year. When we've asked for reasons, we've been surprised. It's usually not that they're too busy, they've lost their interest in church or they feel rejection from friends. Rather they're wrestling with feeling guilty over their sexual enjoyment. Having been taught that sex and guilt go hand in hand, they felt unclean around church people, the church and especially God. How sad it is to warp young people with an improper teaching about sex. When we make the words *sex, sensuous* and *sin* hiss like the cursed serpent, our children will deal with guilt long after they marry. God's only condemnation concerning sex is when it is outside the pact of marriage.

Some time ago, a newly married couple met me (Robert) before an evening church service. They were all smiles, touches and handholds—radiantly happy. "It looks to me as if you're here to worship and praise the Lord and have a good time," I said.

The husband smiled and answered, "Yes, we've been making love all afternoon, and now we've come to church just to rejoice in the privilege of being married."

Happily and loudly I said, "Praise God, how healthy!" In the presence of God, this couple could rejoice in the blessings He had given them. It was Adam and Eve—and God. A husband, a wife and God. This committed combination is acceptable to God and pleasurable to the marriage partners.

The Act of Sex

"Making love," as the act of sexual intercourse is euphemistically called, involves our mental, physical and emotional natures. Since the sex act begins as an act of the will, let's consider what part *the mind* plays. Many of the decisions about the sex act can be settled before marriage. Will you use birth control? If you're both healthy, leaving the choice of having children up to God or to chance nearly guarantees a family. When or if you'll have children is determined by your actions. Making no plans to prevent pregnancy and then turning to abortion as a means of birth control is *not* an option for Christians.

As you're entering marriage, talk over what each of you is expecting from the other in sexual response and performance. Discuss what your sexual standards will be. Without going into great detail, you might discuss your dreams, desires and fantasies, as well as your hang-ups, fears and reservations.

You might even talk about expectations for anticipated frequency. Whom do you expect to initiate sex? In short, be open and honest with your expectations. The purpose for such discussion is not to settle issues but to discover concepts. As the marital relationship grows, most of those initial mental attitudes will modify or be replaced.

As the marriage matures, you will learn to make adjustments, yet the sexual concepts on which your marriage begins may well have an underlying effect on the sexual union throughout your entire marriage. Unquestionably, the marriage partners' sexual concepts will form the foundation of sexual compatibility. Weakness here will dramatically affect the structure of marriage.

The human act of sex, being a decision of the mind rather than a mere response to a biological cycle, allows us the freedom to express ourselves and our love in imaginative ways. Spontaneity and variety can quickly spark a flame. Routine can douse it pretty fast. "It's 10:00 on Friday night, and the kids are in bed, so it's time to have sex." Sound familiar? Use some imagination!

Never forget that the largest sex organ in your body is between your ears. What you think controls your sexual appetite. There are few sexual problems in marriage that don't originate in the brain.

We cannot, of course, discount the physical, biological part of the sex act. Remember that your size, coloring, physical features and the dimensions of your sex organs have virtually nothing to do with your sexuality. Our bodies are the products of our parents. Since we had no control over our genes, it is worthless to be upset because we have "too much" or "too little." The real secret of sexual satisfaction is accepting what you've been given and learning to be a sexual being with what you have, without longing to be different. What counts is not how you're equipped, but how you use the equipment.

Embarrassed over your body? Think of it this way: there are just two kinds of people on the earth, male and female. The differences among males and among females are just that—differences—and different is neither inferior nor superior. It's simply diverse. Actually, the characteristics of your physical body were likely part of what initially caught the attention of your intended husband or wife.

God made us to need each other, and the Bible addresses this physical need: "Let the husband render to his wife the affection due her, and likewise also the wife to her husband. The wife does not have authority over her own body, but the husband does. And likewise the husband does not have authority over his own body, but the wife does. Do not deprive one another except with consent for a time" (1 Corinthians 7:3-5).

Our bodies belong to our mates. In marriage we are giving to each other our very physical beings: "This body of mine now becomes yours." It's a precious gift beyond compare.

We've looked at the mental part of our nature, which deals with sexual attitudes, and our physical being, which deals with bodily action. The third aspect, our *emotional nature*, deals with arousal and its fulfillment. As there are vast physical differences between the natures of men and women, so there are equally great differences between the emotional natures of the two sexes. For instance, the male can be quickly aroused sexually by thought, sight and smell. Most men can climax with relatively little stimulation in comparison with a woman. Sight is less important to her than touch, and word and security coupled with tenderness are vital to her arousal.

Just because the children are in bed, the evening meal is over and the husband brought flowers home doesn't mean that the wife is ready for intercourse. Her emotional nature yearns for more romance than does the masculine. When the household duties are complete and privacy is available, she may warm up to romance. The next move is the man's, but it should not be a direct bee-line to intercourse. The wife needs a little emotional persuasion, a bit of seduction. She needs to hear words of love; she needs to be encouraged and fondled so that her emotions can be released and she can be fulfilled.

Failure to understand this emotional difference between the sexes can greatly disturb, if not destroy, sexual compatibility. These differences are not cultural but innate. They're the way God made us, male and female. A woman's emotional tears, smiles, touches and embraces produce and release the excitement of the created world. She needs to be understood as a highly sensitive person and helped into the sexual experience in a way consistent with her nature.

Many men can complete their sexual experience in a few minutes; then they're satisfied and ready to sleep. In that time, however, the woman is often merely getting started. It may be ten to twenty minutes before her body and mind are ready for complete fulfillment. Another difference is that the husband's sexual desires are satisfied after he has had an ejaculation. But if the husband is a patient lover, the wife can have multiple orgasms Good compatibility in the sex act requires the man to slow down and extend his love, allowing time for the woman to "catch up" with him emotionally. Failure to learn this prompts some husbands to complain they're married to "cold" women. Some years ago I heard it said, "There are no frigid women; only clumsy men."

The wife also needs to bring a patient, understanding spirit to the bedroom, meeting her husband's needs, which may be different from hers. As a rule, a man's desires are more frequent than a woman's, and he wants to climax every time. Many women, however, say they don't need a "gourmet meal" every time they have sex; they're often content with a "sandwich and a Coke"—less than a full orgasm.

Recognizing this difference in sexual desires, a husband should allow his wife to control how much sexual activity she needs at any given time. Otherwise, he may feel guilty for insisting on having sex when she's getting little out of it. A woman's needs can vary in correlation with her monthly cycle. Sometimes she may need more sexual stimulation than other times. Sometimes embracing, holding, touching and fondling will be sufficiently fulfilling to her. Happily married couples will testify there's no bad sex; it's just that some occasions are better than others. Don't compare; enjoy!

The scriptural teaching, "Husbands, love your wives, just as Christ also loved the church and gave Himself for it" (Ephesians 5:25), gives us a point of comparison. Christ loves the church devotedly, sacrificially and with variety. How dull our Christian experience would be if Christ approached us the same way every day, if every contact with Him produced identical responses in us. In reality, one time we are carried to heights of praise; another time we stand in silence and awe; other times we may weep and simply say, "He's here." He is offering us spiritual companionship. In a variety of ways God loves His church. Husbands are urged by God to follow this example.

Sexual compatibility will extend sexual expression throughout the lifetime of a marriage. As we get older, the need for sexual expression declines, but the need for companionship increases—talking, having fellowship, sharing, just enjoying friendship with each other. The sexual relationship needn't die, however. The mind, not the body, cuts off the act of sex. Couples in their eighties often continue to have a sexual relationship. Sex, like good cheese, improves with aging. Like almost everything in life, "practice makes perfect." As the marriage matures, we should be able to tone our abilities and be better at it than when we first married. As exciting as the newness of sex was on the honeymoon, the best sexual relationship will be after we've been married a while, after we've learned how to fulfill each other's needs in the privacy of our bedrooms, doing what we want to do because we have the time and desire to put into it. No matter how long you've been married, the best year of your marriage can be *this* year.

The Tact of Sex

While it's no secret that married couples have inter-course, it is and should be a very private matter. What happens in the bedroom should not be discussed on the golf course or in the ladies' room. If someone comes to you seeking counsel on sexual matters, talk principles, not personal practice. If that person presses for personal details, he or she has ceased wanting counsel and is likely vicariously enjoying your sexual experiences. Refer such a person to a professional counselor. What you and your mate do sexually is the business of no one but the two of you.

Since sex is so much a matter of fantasy, tactfully express to your spouse the changes in mental concepts that come over a period of time. What "turned me on" a year ago may not seem erotic now. Communication is a key to continued sexual compatibility, but be tactful, not condemnatory. Consider how much of a person's ego is wrapped up in his or her sexuality. Ridiculing, harshly criticizing or shaming your partner's sexual performance can destroy the very thing the marriage so desperately needs.

Introduce your children to the sexuality of marriage in a gentle and tactful manner. They need to see warmth of love between mother and father. Probably the greatest gift a father can give his children is consistent love to their mother. Though a closed door to the parents' bedroom should mean "do not enter," maturing children should understand that Mom and Dad do have a sexual relationship. Remember that you are developing your children's concepts of sexuality. Teach them well, and when they get married they are likely to enjoy sexual fulfillment as much as you in your marriage.

If imagination is 90 percent of sex, tact must be the other

10 percent; achieving mutual satisfaction requires both patience and tact. Sexual compatibility requires continued effort, but the work is more than worth it.

Worksheet

Ken and Kathy have just come home from a seven-day vacation. Even though she didn't go to New York, Kathy is happy. She rested and sunned, and she learned to fish. Ken is not happy. Oh, yes, he fished every day and enjoyed teaching Kathy, but one of his fantasies for the vacation was to have sex every night. Out of the seven days, Kathy wanted sex only two nights.

How would you counsel this couple? If this were your marriage, what would you do?

What questions should Ken and Kathy be asking each other?

SEVEN

THE NORTH FOUNDATION

How Important Is Money to Your Marriage?

"Money answers every thing."
—*Ecclesiastes 10:19*

On a day when Julie received a shocking letter saying their credit account was seriously overdue, her husband, Paul, was buying a new car—totally unbeknownst to her. What do you suppose was the tone of their marriage? Author Larry Burkett describes part of their interaction after Paul arrived home.

" 'I feel like I've got to take care of two children instead of one' [Julie said]. 'The bank sent me a note at work today about our VISA account. If we don't pay it, they're going to turn it over for collection. If my boss gets another garnishment, he'll probably fire me.'

" 'Ah, that's stupid, Julie. They can't fire you for that.

And the bill is not that far overdue anyway.'

" 'So I'm stupid now, too, am I?' Julie shouted as she stormed out of the room. 'If I'm that stupid, I guess you should have married somebody else.' She slammed the door to their bedroom, and Paul heard the lock click shut."

Fearful of what Julie would do when she learned about the new car, and knowing she was thinking of leaving him, Paul snuck out of the house and headed for the dealership, hoping to get his old car back.*

In the world's scheme of things, money, not love, "makes the world go 'round." To the wealthy, money is power. Most Americans feel that money is more than desirable; it's an absolute necessity. In the church universal, a faction has always declared money to be evil; poverty is the route to spirituality. Conversely, others have earnestly sought to use spiritual power to attain wealth. And in our society today, money problems are the leading cause of divorce.

The Bible neither condemns nor condones money, but it does warn, "The love of money is a root of all kinds of evil, for which some have strayed from the faith in their greediness, and pierced themselves through with many sorrows" (1 Timothy 6:10).

In reality, money is not the force that causes earth to rotate, nor is it power. Money is a medium of exchange that represents you, its holder. Money is *you* in foldable form. You have exchanged your brains or brawn for this thing called money, and that money represents you on deposit or in an exchangeable form. In agrarian cultures, the barter system is often used to obtain needed goods or services. In industrial societies, this becomes too complex, so we trade our services for money and in turn exchange that money for the goods or services we desire.

---

* Larry Burkett, *Debt-Free Living* (Chicago: Moody, 1989), p. 21.

Considering this background information, Oswald J. Smith once declared, "I have learned that money is not the measure of a man, but it is often the means of finding out how small he is."

We have long held that, if we can observe how people handle money, we will learn what they think about themselves, for that money *is* them.

Concepts of Money

Years ago, when I (Robert) was selling insurance, I was taught the following patter: "Perhaps you've never thought of this, but every day that you work, you exchange a certain amount of your energy, intelligence and capabilities for a certain amount of money. This process goes on all through your life until you find that you're no longer able to work, no longer need to work or have no desire to work. By that time, if you haven't saved up your past energies in the form of money, you'll be dependent upon someone else."

As you may have guessed, that was the beginning of a sales talk about a retirement plan, but there's truth to it. You work for money; you earn it, and it's a reflection of your very life.

How different it was decades ago, when a person's work enlarged herds of cattle, increased acreage under cultivation and built houses. Such assets were passed from generation to generation. Now all this has been reduced to green paper: M-O-N-E-Y. How could this not become an important part of marriage?

You may have heard it said: don't talk about money. It's the one topic that gets people upset faster than any other. When you touch a person's pocketbook, you touch his or her emotional buttons.

More family arguments have probably occurred over money matters than any other issue. But the problem is rarely the abundance or absence of money; it's the way the money is handled by the partners in the marriage. Young couples are often taken by surprise. Individually, each handled money successfully. But after the wedding, conflict follows conflict, and many are rooted in the diverse concepts the partners hold about money.

All too frequently, Mister Tightwad marries Sister Spendthrift, which soon leads to an open declaration of war. Again, their problem is not money. (He has plenty.) Their problem is their differing views of the fundamental purpose of money. He sees the acquisition of money as an ultimate goal. Her goal is the acquisition of tangible things. He views money as an end; she sees it as a means to an end.

Money should always be viewed as a means to an end, as a way of getting what we need or want. When the possession of money itself is a life goal, life can grow icy cold. As Bonhours said over a hundred years ago, "Money is a good servant, but a poor master."

Surely you've heard stories of poverty-ridden people living for years in squalor. Then, after they die, vast quantities of money are found hidden in their dingy, dismal rooms. They sacrificed living for money. They found their sense of accomplishment in money rather than seeing money as a means to help them live comfortably.

The way men and women display their money is evidence of their differing attitudes about it. We've seen men pull out a roll of money with a hundred dollar bill on top—and singles underneath. But how many times have you seen a woman reach into her purse, take out a wad of money and count out the big bills? Similarly, watch five men go into a restaurant to eat. One of them—the "big shot"—is likely to declare, "I'll pick up the check!" To impress the waitress and his companions, he'll pull the largest bill out of his wallet or money clip, and he'll often overtip the waitress. He's bucking for a "Hey, he's really something!" from his friends. When five women dine together and get the check, however, they're far more apt to divide the bill to the exact penny of each person's order. They may even pay for it individually at the cashier—even if people line up impatiently behind them.

What's going on here? Men are more apt to think of money as power, while women think of money as possessions. In either case, money can become a liability rather than an asset.

In the fall of 1936, the town of Bandon, Oregon, was destroyed by a forest fire gone wild. Our father, who pastored a church in that town, saved the lives of his family by taking us to the beach. We stood in the water part of the night. The rest of the night we buried our heads in the wet sand as protection against the thick, hot smoke. If memory serves correctly, thirteen people died in that fire. Of that number, ten were women trying to save their possessions. One woman was found dead in her front yard next to the charred remains of her refrigerator, which she had wrestled there from her kitchen. We don't know where she thought she could put it. It was too big to fit in her car, but she apparently thought, This is my possession, and I must save it.

The same principle is sometimes evident in the breakup of a marriage. A man might place all his possessions in the trunk of his car, while the wife needs a moving van. On the other hand, he may maintain control of the bulk of the couple's money. These contrasts serve to illustrate the differing ways we are taught to view and handle money. Concepts count.

Conflicts in Money Management

Bring into a marriage a man with one point of view toward money and a woman with an entirely different view, and you can expect conflict. The young wife may have worked for several years, earning her own money. If she has been living at home with her parents, she may have used her salary to purchase clothing, personal items and a car without feeling the weight of financial responsibility.

When she enters into marriage, she now faces the demands of a household. Every time she turns around, there is expense, expense, expense. The new husband tends to nag, "Watch what you spend; it costs so much to live."

The wife, used to a wide range of financial liberty, cries, "There's never anything left over for what I want to buy," and her claim is true. There are the rent, utilities, groceries, two car payments.... The feeling that all the work goes just to keep them alive is taxing to both husband and wife.

The initial shock of this financial burden can be greatly lessened if the marriage has a strong and supportive foundation of communication. The financial structure of any marriage needs to be discussed again and again.

In marriage there's no place for secretiveness about money. Harmony demands open discussion, including what each has in capabilities, assets and liabilities. This discussion needs to begin before the marriage. There should be no financial surprises on or after the wedding night.

Why not sit down before the wedding and lay it all out? Men, tell her how much you make per month, how much tax and other deductions come out of this, and what your actual take-home pay is. Women, do the same. This is what you will have to live on. Love is great, but it doesn't put much food on the table.

Perhaps it will be evident that the two of you cannot live on one salary. "Two can live as cheaply as one" is true only if one is willing to go without eating. Perhaps the wife-to-be will say, "Well, I'll get (or keep) a job, and I'll pay for this and that." That's fine, but it would be better to calculate, "My take-home pay is x, and your take-home pay will be y, and when we add them together we have a total monthly income of z. That's the amount we'll have to live on every month."

If the husband's wages are sufficient to meet the household budget but the wife chooses to continue working for a while, we recommend that her salary be identified for specific projects. Perhaps she'll work until a child comes or until a certain bill is paid or until a down payment has been made on a house. But let the wife's money be set aside for a purpose for a short period of time, and let the man feel that it is his job to support his wife. This is a necessary fulfillment of his manhood.

The earlier you can move from "my money" and "your money" to "our money," the sooner you will begin to work harmoniously on the foundation of finances. "His" and "hers" have to become "ours," with all secrets about money evaporating.

Not being secretive about money doesn't mean, however, that mates don't honor each other's privacy. Early in our marriage, my (Robert's) wife learned that I don't like anyone, including her, to get into my wallet. At night, I take my wallet out of my pocket and lay it on my dresser. The next morning I expect to find it just the way I left it. It's not that there's anything in my wallet I would be ashamed for her to see. I carry just a few credit cards, some business cards and a little money. There are no secrets, no private telephone numbers. The reason for my desire of privacy? That wallet is me. It is my one possession that my wife doesn't wash, dust or fix. It's *mine,* and my wife is wise to respect this.

Similarly, men should respect the privacy of their wives. If I ask my wife for something and she says, "It's in my brown purse," I go get her brown purse and bring it to her. I don't hunt through it myself. Her purse is her private possession, and so is everything in it. She knows how much

I make, and I know how much it takes to operate the household. Even though there are no secrets, we still respect each other's privacy in the handling of that money.

Constructing a Budget

As dull as the word *budget* may sound, one of the best ways to prevent or resolve conflicts in money management is to plan a budget for the first year of marriage. It's practical, and it will work.

Having already determined the gross and take-home income of the family, consider the expenditures. The first calculation is to subtract 10 percent of the income for the tithe that belongs to God—the first fruits of your labor. The quickest way to avert financial trouble is to give the first fruits to God without question. Bring it to the house of the Lord where you worship, and put it in the offering. This involves you in a divine law and principle, and it involves God in your financial endeavors. In the very last book of the Old Testament, God said,

> Bring all the tithes into the storehouse,
> That there may be food in My house,
> And try Me now in this,
> Says the Lord of hosts,
> If I will not open for you the windows of heaven
> And pour out for you such blessing
> That there will not be room enough to receive it!
> (Malachi 3:10)

God has pledged that if we bring Him the tenth, He will bring us an abundance.

Your immediate reaction may be, Now I've reduced my spending money by 10 percent. No, not really. Make your budget on the basis of "tithe subtracted is tithe added."

What you actually do is add that 10 percent to the amount with which you started. Instead of saying, I had $1,000 and gave $100, so now I have $900, add the $100 to the $1,000 and now figure your whole budget at $1,100. It will work. God will give back to you, pressed down, running over. You can count on it.

There's an additional simple psychological value to tithing. Giving God the first fruits of our incomes makes us very money-aware. When we're conscious of the amount of money available, we become more cautious in how we spend it, and that concern, plus the abundance God gives, increases our spending power.

Having set aside God's share, the next move is to make a list of what it costs to live: housing, utilities, food, clothing, car payment, insurance and so on. Keep it open. Make allowances for recreation and play, and always have a place for unexpected expenses. Even at the beginning of the marriage, when funds are probably at their lowest level, try to budget a small percent of the income for savings. This habit will pay big dividends in the future. Another budget item often overlooked by young couples is a personal fund for each partner. Neither the wife nor the husband should have to ask the other for money. Set aside equal amounts for two private funds, his and hers, of which there need be no accounting. One spouse may want to save up his or her share to buy something, give it to someone or spend it frivolously. No matter, the other person should not have a voice in how it is used.

The four-letter word *fair* is of utmost importance when it comes to money. One partner shouldn't get the benefit of money while the other is left out. If there's money for golf clubs for him, there should also be money for a new coat for her. Perhaps it won't be in the same month, but such details can be worked out by prior agreement.

If we hired the finest accountant in the land to prepare

a tailor-made budget for us, it would be useful only if it were implemented. Budgets must be more than suggestions; they're the guidelines for a household's financial security. Regardless of the discipline required, they must be followed. If they're not, financial chaos can fall far more suddenly than you can imagine. A budget is not meant to keep you from enjoying life; its purpose is to undergird that enjoyment today, tomorrow and into the future.

Credit or Cash?

No one needs to start married life with all the things Mother and Father had after twenty-five or thirty years of marriage, though that seems to be the common expectation these days. You will probably start with far less, simply because you're young and it takes years to accumulate possessions. Most couples have less money available in the first year or two of marriage than at any other time of their lives together. Why try to have everything at the beginning? You'll have nothing toward which to work. There's no hurry. Slow down and enjoy having less. It's amazing how much you appreciate having things you worked for instead of working for the things you have.

Happy is the couple that ignores the financial scheme of the federal government and resists borrowing from the future to enjoy living today. If you're running up credit card bills and using time-payment plans to purchase furniture, you're spending future money in the present. When the future comes, you'll have no money to spend. Furthermore, the interest on those credit payments makes your purchases far more costly.

Some of the finest words you can learn to say in the early months of marriage are, "No, thank you. We can't afford it now." You won't have to say no to the creditors if you say no to the credit pushers. Credit unions, banks and furniture stores eagerly await couples who walk in and say, "We're getting married, and we'd like to establish credit." Remember, credit is good until it's abused, at which time it will rise up and swallow you. You no longer use it; it uses you. As someone wisely said, "When your outgo exceeds your income, your upkeep is your downfall."

As a young couple, pretend you've been married two or three years. What does that mean? Drive a two-year-old car. Purchase used furniture. Buy a used washing machine from the want ads. Once it's installed in a dark corner of the washroom, a new machine's shiny chrome and blinking lights don't mean a thing anyway. The purpose of a washing machine is to wash clothes. So what if it's secondhand? It does the job, and it was brand new just two or three years ago. To purchase it new would cost three hundred to five hundred dollars, but that same machine will sell for one hundred dollars or less after two or three years.

Stay as far away from payment plans as you possibly can. Buy what you can afford at the time. As the old Amish proverb says, "Spend less than you earn and you'll never be in debt." Monthly payments become a chain around the neck so that you can't go where you'd like or do what you'd like; all your cash is committed to the things you're paying off. You can enjoy possessions when you're older, when the appetite for going and doing is lessened and replaced with the joy of having. When young couples try to do and have at the same time, the financial stress often leads to failure. Build memories of trips and dinners and activities now; let "having" come later, when you've slowed down your pace and enjoy a better income.

Young people who instead work to buy the boat, the RV or the big house with a swimming pool find that afterward they're not content. Why? Because they're in the "doing" time of their lives. Live *on* less and *with* less in order to have more freedom to do things and go places.

Jesus said, "Where your treasure is, there your heart will be also" (Matthew 6:21). In this context, *heart* speaks of the emotions. It's always dangerous to have our treasure in finances or possessions rather than in our relationships—with God, our marriage partners, our families and our friends. Remember the story of the rich young ruler? He came to Jesus wanting to know how to get into His kingdom. When Jesus recited several of the Ten Commandments, the young man assured Jesus that he had done all those things from his youth. Jesus then put His finger on the man's problems: sell your possessions, and distribute them to the poor. This man's affections were in finances and possessions, not in relationships with people. The Bible tells us he went away sorrowful and unwilling to part with his riches. But a call to poverty is not the moral of the lesson. Jesus was teaching that we should seek the kind of treasure that brings joy and not sorrow.

Continuing Your Concepts

The car at the pole position likely takes the lead in the Indianapolis 500 auto race, but that doesn't make that driver the winner. The winning money goes to the driver who crosses the finish line first. Between the starting gun and the finish flag lie grueling miles of competitive driving, pit stops and dangerous traffic. Similarly, the financial foundation of a marriage must extend beyond the first year or two. The long haul calls for advance preparation, constant teamwork and consistent application of the rules of finance that have been agreed upon. Once a budget has been established and made workable, the next step is to acknowledge your capabilities with money.

Though we should never set money as a high priority in life, a weakness of many Christian households is a lack of financial goals. It's wise to recognize where you are now financially, and it's equally wise to set some goals toward which to work. Make some projections showing where the two of you will be a year from now and five years from now. If you don't know where you're going, you'll never know when you arrive. If you have no financial plans in your future, you'll tend to exhaust all your money in the present.

Don't make money your goal; make it your servant as you set your goals in the good things of life. Establish goals in terms of things you wish to attain and places you wish to go. Yes, you'll need money to do those things, but money is not the goal. You're aiming for the success in doing, in being and in having. John Wesley, the founder of Methodism, said of money, "Get all you can; save all you can; give all you can." No one has improved on that formula.

At one particular camp meeting, more than three hundred thousand dollars were pledged for missions. To those were added more than one hundred thousand dollars for home missions. Four hundred thousand dollars? Fantastic! Where did it all come from? From people who set goals of making money *so they could give toward the spreading of the gospel.*

Few have explored the pleasure found in being able to give to the kingdom of God. It is more than the gift of money; it's an expression of ourselves—an opportunity to transmit ourselves into ministry through giving of ourselves in the foldable form—money. We may never go to Africa to preach, but sharing our finances with one who does answer that call makes us a partner in the spreading of the good news of God's forgiving grace through Jesus Christ.

Paul challenged the Ephesian elders to "remember the words of the Lord Jesus, that He said, 'It is more blessed to give than to receive' " (Acts 20:35). If Jesus said it and Paul emphasized it, it must be true.

Too often there is a great gap between desiring to give

and actually giving. We've seen that when you ask a congregation, "How many of you would be willing to give a hundred or a thousand dollars to underwrite this ministry?" You can count on many hands being raised. But when you ask, "How many are now able to give that amount?" very few hands go up. More are willing than able. Will you accept our challenge to set a financial goal of being able to respond to those needs the Holy Spirit quickens to your heart?

Naturally, those who have money are constantly sought after by those who do not. Some people live well by projecting guilt onto those who have worked well and earned a decent income. Just as it is wiser to teach people to fish than to give them free fish, so it is better to tell a person, "I can help you financially as long as you're helping yourself." Share what you learn about how to earn money. Help others to work toward self-supporting financial health.

If you do well with your money, recognize that God gave you a stewardship for the advancement of the kingdom. To every faithful steward, God promises abundance, strength, protection, guidance and instruction.

Faithful stewardship of your funds must extend to your children. In this generation, America's riches have almost killed our children's integrity. It's natural to desire that our children have more than we had. But if, in giving this to them, we destroy their moral character, we have cursed rather than blessed them.

Every youth has a right to the opportunities of America, but it is incumbent upon us to see that our children work to develop those rights. They shouldn't live exclusively off the family finances but learn to work for what they need and, especially, want—starting in childhood.

It takes time to teach children the value of money, and it often requires "tough" love.

When my (Robert's) youngest daughter finished school and went to work, her mother helped her prepare a budget that included funds for gasoline and lunches. All went well the first month, but a week before payday of the second month, she said, "Mom, I need some lunch money. I have just enough money left to fill the gas tank so I can go to work."

"Then you'll either have to pack a lunch and take it with you or go hungry," Shirley told her.

Lynette thought her mother was being mean and selfish, but she learned to handle her money better after that.

Some parents sacrifice severely so their children can meet an artificial social standard. But that's not fair to anyone in the family. Let the children know that a share of Father's paycheck is set aside for them, but there are others who share in that check as well. Openness and fairness in the handling of family finances prevent family strife. True openness includes passing on to a new generation the principles of earning. If it isn't learned in the home, where will it be learned?

The financial foundation of a home is as vital as the other foundations. If all are firmly established and correctly built upon, a home can stand any storm that blows.

Worksheet

Ken and Kathy enjoyed their vacation last year because they had it in their budget. This year the budget allowed for a similar vacation, but unexpectedly the used car, used washer, used dryer and used refrigerator all needed repairs—repairs that cost more than was budgeted for two years. Ken and Kathy had to use their savings and dip into their vacation and Christmas funds.

Friends are telling Ken and Kathy to charge their vacation this year; they both deserve the time away because they've worked so hard. Besides, Ken can get a part-time job to pay off the charges or work overtime on Sundays.

How would you advise this couple regarding their vacation budget?

EIGHT

MAINTAINING THE HOUSE

Repair Rather Than Replacement

"A threefold cord is not quickly broken."
—Ecclesiastes 4:12

Jennifer was young and deeply hurt. "My husband is having an affair," she told me (Robert). "I'm going to divorce him."

When I talked with her husband, I found him embarrassed at having been exposed, but he wasn't truly repentant. His passion for the other woman had not abated, and he resented his wife's belligerent attitude toward him. I was unsuccessful in saving their marriage.

Many months later, Jennifer remarried. Although this new husband never cheated on her sexually, he was undependable as a breadwinner, and he preferred activities outside the home far more than he appreciated his home and new family. I spent many months counseling the couple. I couldn't believe the amount of emotional abuse Jennifer took from her new husband. One day she told me, "If I had been half as patient with my first husband, I think I could have saved the marriage. I've determined to make this marriage work at any cost."

We Americans lust after the new. It matters little how well our cars are running; when the new models are introduced, we want one. We have become a disposable society. Just look at the tons of throwaway items daily hauled to dump sites. Replacement rather than repair is our philosophy.

When traveling through Europe, we have been impressed with the age of many of the buildings. We've stayed in houses that were several hundred years old. We've crossed bridges in Holland built before Columbus discovered America. Those structures were not only built well, but they've also been maintained carefully so that they're still useful.

Such is not the case in most of America. We build for the short haul. A fifty-year-old structure may be destroyed to make room for something new. Perhaps this reflects our continuing affluence, or maybe it pictures the minimal care we give a thing once we have obtained it.

Whatever the reasons, we're reared with an attitude: if it's broken, replace it. Tragically, we bring that same philosophy into human relationships. We treat friendships as disposable commodities. We even prefer to destroy an ailing marriage and replace it rather than repair the damages. The needless cost in emotional suffering, financial deprivation, insecurity for the children and loneliness for all parties involved is incalculable.

Some marriages should never have been entered into in the first place. Some divorces are not only justified but essential for the safety of the abused. We have observed, however, that most people who divorce and remarry have to work much harder at the second marriage than they would have had to work to *repair* the first marriage. When counseling we've repeatedly heard, "If I had known then what I know now, I would never have agreed to a divorce."

Divorce is not a quick fix. Many times it fixes nothing. Neither is it cheap. Over the years, the price of separation is often paid again and again. It may be a doorway of escape from present pain, but it leads to a long, narrow hallway of continued pain that tends to compound.

Any homeowner can tell you that the thrill of home ownership is accompanied by the expense of maintenance. Roofs have to be replaced. Trees have to be trimmed or removed. Sewer lines have to be unclogged, and repainting comes around all too frequently. Wind damage can require complete renovation of a section of the house. There's nothing glamorous about making repairs, but fixing the damages to the house immediately as they occur preserves that home for us.

The marriage house does not need to be bulldozed when it begins to lean to one side. Foundations can be rebuilt. You may have been beaten by a serious storm, but repair will be far less costly than replacement. An experienced builder may not only repair a damaged house, but also update and modernize it. Similarly, with the guidance of a qualified counselor, many damaged marriages have been more than just repaired; they have been upgraded and made far more livable.

Repair, enlargement and modernization are messy activities that don't come cheaply to either housing or marriages, but they are far preferable to replacement. Furthermore, you have pleased the Lord, before whom you vowed to love your spouse till death do you part.

FIVE FOUNDATIONS FOR MARRIAGE

Inspection—Checkup

At one point as a pastor, I (Judson) oversaw the building of a new sanctuary, which the members of the congregation constructed with their own hands. As time went on, I grew so attached to and spent so much time in that building that I failed to see its faults or need for repairs. So I devised a plan: at least quarterly, I would ask a guest with an outgoing personality if he or she could give me fifteen minutes. I'd pick up a clipboard and conduct a rapid tour of our facilities, asking my guest to point out anything that needed correction. I was always amazed that the person could see burned-out bulbs, torn carpet, scuffed walls and even cracked windows to which I had grown accustomed. Seeing the building through another's eyes filled a page with items that needed to be repaired.

Perhaps we need to make a similar checkup on our marriages. It's easy to take our relationships for granted and not see the worn or broken places. Sometimes merely talking with our partners will unfold areas that need special attention. Other times we may need to see our marriages through the eyes of a close acquaintance or a counselor. Even if this inspection costs a little time and money, it would still be far cheaper than divorce and remarriage.

Not all inspections require an expert, however. A home owner can stand back and look at the roof of his or her house and see that the shingles need replacement. Reroofing at this point would prove to be much cheaper than to wait until the roof leaks and ruins the ceilings. Similarly, our own marriages afford us many things to inspect.

Do you express your love for your partner as you did early in the marriage, or do you assume that he or she knows how much you love? To be kept fresh, love needs to be expressed. If it's awkward or embarrassing to say, "I love you," your covenant of love likely needs some repair work.

How well are the two of you communicating? Are you merely saying words, or are you actually conversing with each other? Do you really know what your partner does with his or her day? We have counseled women who couldn't even name their husbands' professions. They merely knew that he "went to the office." What are your partner's dreams or ambitions? He or she may have told you, but were you listening?

It's also important to check on the spiritual concepts of your spouse from time to time. One's ideas do change. Is it possible that your partner has matured spiritually without your observation? Or you may have grown spiritually without bringing your partner along with you.

While family backgrounds don't change as the marriage ages, your relationship to those backgrounds should mature; your understanding of actions rooted in that background should increase. Are you still as irritated as you used to be over the toothpaste tube's being squeezed from the middle? How about the attitudes you had toward his or her parents? The years should have mellowed your opinions and made you more tolerant of your in-laws. Check yourself.

Similarly, inspect your sexual compatibility, for sex needs change as a relationship matures. Sexual attraction often brings two people together, but through the years, you come to like as well as need each other. The pressures of life, the strain of raising children, physical weaknesses and even the aging process often diminish the force of the sex drive. Are you sensitive to those changes in your partner?

Attitudes toward money also need to be checked regularly. As income changes and household needs are met, money often becomes available for luxuries. Is this surplus being shared equally? Have you made quality provisions for the future, or are you spending everything you earn?

Those five areas, the fundamental foundations for marriage, need to be inspected regularly. If weaknesses, cracks or failures are discovered, they can be corrected. If strengths are observed, they can be built upon.

The story is told of the teenager who made deliveries for the corner drugstore after school. After a few weeks of work, he phoned the manager. With a disguised voice, he tried to apply for the job of delivery boy.

"I already have a delivery boy," the manager said.

"Is he satisfactory?" the teenager asked.

"Completely," the manager answered.

Hanging up the phone, the lad went about his duties with a new sense of satisfaction and security. He had checked up on himself and found he was succeeding. Maybe we need to do the same sort of checkup on our marriages.

Implementation—Fix Up

Some years ago, I (Judson) purchased a home that frequently had water in the basement. Unable to find the source of the problem, I called in specialists who made a series of recommendations. But the water problem wasn't solved until I implemented those recommendations. Knowing the problem wasn't sufficient. I had to spend the necessary money and expend the time and energy to fix it.

Seeing a weakness in your marriage will only compound your sense of guilt unless you do something to repair the damage. Have you discovered a weakness in expressing your love to your partner? Deliberately begin to speak your love. You'll be amazed at how it can reinforce your sense of love. Beyond merely saying, "I love you," make yourself *demonstrate* your love. Don't wait for the chance to do something "big" either. Love is best demonstrated in little ways like a smile, a kind word or a chore done without having to be asked.

If inspection shows a breakdown in communication, the

only answer is to talk to each other. It may seem difficult at first, but deliberate action will get the communication going. The longer you wait, the more painful the penalties will be and the more difficult the task will become. Turn off the television set and talk to each other. Start the conversation on a level at which you have been comfortable talking, and then slowly bring the conversation to deeper issues. Practice being a good listener. Conversation is give and take. When one party dominates the discussion, the dialogue has become a monologue. Marriage is not giving and receiving orders; it's the sharing of two lives. This will require nearly equal time in all communications.

Spiritual concepts can be kept on an even level when the two of you pursue your spiritual life together. Going to church as a family, reading the Bible and praying together and even talking about spiritual things will strengthen the spiritual foundation of the home and introduce the children to the concepts of the parents. When every family member shares his or her spiritual life with the others, a common faith is established in the home.

If the foundation of family background is sinking, shore it up with the reinforcement of understanding, acceptance and tolerance. Bring resentments to the surface, and deal with them honestly. Sometimes a third party can help in overcoming problems produced by the vast differences in family backgrounds. If you will pay to have the family car fixed, why not invest some money in family counseling? After all, if the Lord grants you long life, your marriage and family should long outlive your automobile. If the budget is too strained to pay a counselor, a good pastor will often give short-term guidance in repairing family relationships.

Complete sexual compatibility may be impossible to achieve. As soon as you think things couldn't be better, you realize the relationship needs to be fine-tuned. At whatever point one of the partners becomes insensitive to the needs of the other, compatibility is threatened. Since sex is often the glue that holds the marriage together, or at least the oil that keeps the gears lubricated, it dare not be ignored or taken for granted. If the checkup reveals weaknesses in this area, work on them. If outside help is needed, seek it. This part of a relationship does not simply correct itself.

The money foundation needs to be bolstered regularly, as it undergirds so many marital activities. Constantly remind yourself that the way money is managed, not the amount available, determines the success or failure of this foundation. Happy is the home that has learned to reverse the trend of running into debt and crawling out.

Where both partners are willing to work together, any marriage can be fixed. It may take great effort and much forgiveness, but the family home of marriage *can* be repaired if you're willing to tackle the task of working from the foundation up.

Improvement—Spruce Up

Sound foundations are essential. But that doesn't mean we have to stop there. Even sound houses can be improved. Frequently families enlarge their existing house rather than sell and move to another. Sometimes a paint job, new wallpaper and fresh carpeting can restore the glory of an old house.

Similarly, even good marriages should be worked on. Most marriages can be enlarged; the coming of children often forces this enlargement. Some of the freshness of the original marriage can be brought back with the equivalent of paint and wallpaper. Dare to make changes that improve your marriage. If you were especially young when you married, your maturity should make it possible to spruce up your marriage and make it even more desirable than it was when the wedding march still echoed in your ears.

Your marriage can wear out, get shabby, stale and dated, or you can invest the time and energy to update it. Change doesn't require a new person in the marriage; it just requires improving the relationship between the two partners. As you remember to check up, fix up and spruce up your marriage year upon year, you can grow old enjoying the family structure you have lovingly tended.

Our father lost his mother early in his teens. His father did not remarry until both the boys had left the farm. Following his sons from Kentucky to California, he met a widow named Mary and married her. A better match could hardly have been made.

We knew them in their aging years. They lived in a small house on the corner of an almond orchard in Esparto, California, where Grandpa pastored a small congregation of elderly people.

We children looked forward to our monthly visit in their home. Grandpa and Grandma were like two peas in a pod. Whatever one did, the other also did. With their declining physical strength, it often took the two of them to make one whole person. This was especially true when they would go places in a car. Grandma was the original backseat driver, but Grandpa needed and accepted it.

It was almost impossible to visit in their home without being urged to stay for a delicious, farm-style meal, after which Grandpa read the Bible and offered spirited thanksgiving to God for the simplest provisions of life.

With their days of productive work behind them, they spent their final years enjoying one another, sharing friendships and fellowshipping with God in His Word. As boys, we became convinced that marriage can be even more meaningful in old age than in youth.

"Grow old along with me! The best is yet to be" (Robert Browning).

Worksheet

Ken and Kathy have been married a few years now, and they notice they've lost the romance they once had. Deeper than that, Ken is beginning to feel that he doesn't love Kathy anymore. Even though he desires her sexually, he really doesn't like her.

Kathy is bothered by the fact that other men at church are catching her eye. She notices especially the ones who are more spiritual than Ken. Why can't Ken be as sensitive to the needs of her heart as Brother Bill?

Is this marriage worth saving? If so, what can Kathy do to rediscover her sensitive husband? What can Ken do to "like" his wife again beyond just the physical contact?

NINE

WHEN YOU HAVE TO REBUILD

Foundations
for Remarriage

*"I thank my God always concerning you for the grace
of God which was given to you by Christ Jesus."*
—*1 Corinthians 1:4*

A gnes was a happy homemaker and a fulfilled mother. In her eyes, the sun rose and set with her husband, John. When an automobile accident took him out of her life, her world came crashing down around her. Life became a nightmare. For months she struggled against depression. She lacked commercial job skills, and besides, the three small children needed the security of her presence.

Frank, an older gentleman in her church, began to reach out sympathetically to her. She found that just being with a caring man relieved her anxieties. When Frank proposed marriage only six months after John's death, Agnes felt this must be God's provision for her, and she accepted.

It wasn't long before she realized that Frank wasn't at all like John. Rather than accept this as fact, however, she kept comparing Frank's every action with her memory of John. By the time they brought their problem to me, it was too late for a solution. Frank was hurt to the point of hopelessness.

"I can't compete with her dead husband," he said. "John must have been an archangel."

Agnes admitted that she was still deeply in love with her deceased husband and just could not respond positively to Frank, although she deeply appreciated and respected him. They divorced, adding guilt to her already heavy load of loneliness. She hadn't worked her way through the ending of her first marriage before entering the second. Clearly, second marriages bring with them a whole new set of challenging issues.

As married men we have experienced most of what we've written so far. When we write about remarriage, however, we leave the familiar fields of experience and enter a world we have only observed from a distance. Being happily married to our first wives, we have never experienced the trauma of divorce or the death of a mate. Yet, as experienced pastor-counselors, we have held the hands of many persons suffering the pain of a broken relationship. From what we've seen, we would like to share a few principles that may give you courage to love and be loved again.

Back in 1770, Samuel Johnson, a famous English clergyman, spoke of second marriage as the "triumph of hope over experience." Thank God for the triumph of hope! Although a higher percentage of second marriages fail than first marriages, we have nonetheless seen many successful second and even third marriages. It is possible to love and be loved again, especially as we learn to put Christ in the center.

The first thing we want to say to those who are looking toward remarriage is that we grieve with you over the loss of your mate—whether your marriage ended in death or divorce. In either case, your pain was and is real. A part of you was pulled out of the garden of your life, leaving a gaping hole in the soil. You can either build a memorial to this hole or plant something in it.

For those who have lost a partner to death, remember, your partner died, not you. Of course a part of you died with him or her, but most of your being is very much alive. The New Testament teaches that marriage vows are binding only during the life of the partner. In speaking of the release death brings to the marriage vows, Paul stated that the widow was free to be married to any man she chose, as long as he, too, was in the Lord (see 1 Corinthians 7:39). If the widow is free to choose another marriage partner, then certainly the widower is equally free. It does not require divine approval. The permission has already been granted in God's Word.

For the most part, however, this chapter is directed to those who have been divorced, for they don't have the same divine permission the widow and widower have been given. We would be less than honest if we denied the clear teaching of the Scriptures about divorce. The prophet declared without hesitation, "The Lord God of Israel says that He hates divorce" (Malachi 2:16). But the Bible is also clear in authorizing divorce under certain circumstances (see, for example, Matthew 5:32; 1 Corinthians 7:12-15); and if people are free to divorce in those situations, it follows that they're also free to remarry. Even those who divorce their spouses for unbiblical reasons and then remarry can still be forgiven.

Although in grace God forgives all confessed sin, that does not immediately erase the consequences of the sin. Just as wild oats sown will be wild oats reaped, even though

God forgives the act of sowing, so the grace of God that releases a person from the guilt of divorce does not automatically correct the problems that led to the divorce. Few divorces are entirely the fault of one partner. Until you have examined the reasons your first marriage failed, it is dangerous to embark on a second. Even if you did all you could to save the marriage, the breakup has created great pain; it may well have produced self-hatred and a tremendous loss of self-worth. Your anger, frustration and rejection need to be worked through before you embrace another partner.

We plead with you to resist the temptation to remarry with the expectation that the new marriage will dissolve the old pain and loss of self-esteem. That was Agnes's mistake. Give yourself time to lay to rest that previous relationship.

As difficult as it may be, the first covenantal relationship must be surrendered before entering into a second. You cannot serve two masters; the first master has to be given up and the new master honored if a marriage is going to succeed. As long as you find yourself with the deep longing—"I wish I had him or her back"—you are not ready for remarriage. You need to join Paul in saying, "One thing I do, forgetting those things which are behind and reaching forward to those things which are ahead, I press toward the goal" (Philippians 3:13-14).

Complications in the Present

We don't mean to be rude, but let us remind you that the first time you married, you were younger—perhaps much younger. It was no doubt easier for you to adjust to your partner and his or her needs. In the single life of your youth, you had an appetite for the fulfillment available in marriage. When you married, you stepped into a new role and ceased being a single person. Now that your marriage has ended, you've become a single person again; but it's different now, isn't it? You don't feel single in the same way you did before. You made so many adjustments in your married life that you find it impossible to go back to what you were as a single person. And yet you *are* single. Because your mate is no longer with you, you lack the security, the emotional input and even the physical involvement that marriage afforded.

The adjustment to the single life was painful and even threatening at times, but you made it. Now, however, you're marrying again and are facing the need to make another major adjustment. Don't expect this new situation to be any easier. Changes may involve pain, frustration and insecurity, but such is the price for the joys of marriage. Because of what you've been through, and because much of the resilience of youth has been exhausted, it's just not reasonable to expect to make this new adjustment as rapidly as you made it in your first marriage. Even your inexperience worked for you the first time around. You probably allowed a lot of things to roll off your back that won't be so easily dismissed this time. You may not have demanded fulfillment in some areas, and you may be saying, I won't let that happen again. Perhaps you shouldn't let old patterns repeat, but recognize that all the adjustments the second time around will be much slower. Plan to invest the needed time.

Your emotions are like an elastic band: you can stretch them and expect them to come back again and again, but there are just so many stretches in them. Your emotions can be stretched just so many times, and then they will no longer respond. When you're young, you're able to stretch easily. As you get older, the stretch isn't there, so make as few major adjustments as you have to, and make them slowly.

Not only are you older and far more experienced this time around, but you may have children from that first marriage who will certainly affect the relationship in the second marriage. First, children make it almost impossible to sever completely the relationship with your former mate. He or she was also awarded some rights to the children. More than that, divorce from the spouse does not include divorce from the grandparents. Not only will the children want to continue relating to the grandparents, but they'll also have a new set of grandparents when you remarry. This is complicated enough, but relationships are even more complicated if the person you're planning to marry also has children.

Love is a conquering force, of course, but enter the second marriage expecting some conflict; the family backgrounds will clash. In your first marriage, you dealt with the conflict of heredity and diverse family backgrounds on a one-to-one basis. Consider the clash that can erupt when two people marry, each having come through a dissolved marriage and bringing into one household children from both former marriages. It's no longer two people learning to adjust; it's two complete families. It's going to require some quality interpersonal dynamics to make it work.

We are not suggesting you should not marry because of this. We are saying you need to measure what you are entering into. The man who falls in love with the woman who has a family also falls in love with that family. It would be highly unusual for the loyalties of the new wife to transfer completely to her new husband if he emotionally rejected her children. Her loyalties will always be with her children, flesh of her flesh. The bond between them is protective and strong. When an "outsider" comes into this family, he will either accept the unit or the unit will reject him.

During the joy of courtship, children may not seem to be a problem, as they're seen only occasionally and are usually at their best. After the wedding, however, those children will be ever present—in good times and bad. They will interfere in your relationship and compete for your affections. Both of you will have to learn to live with this strained situation. The stories of the wicked stepmother or the mean stepfather surely have their roots in the frustrations of rearing another's children.

Some persons have ruled out a second marriage because of their children. But kids are resilient as long as they know they're loved. Besides, you can't just ignore your own needs. You do have to weigh what kind of parent to your children a potential spouse would be, though.

Joan was barely forty when her husband died, leaving her with a ten-year-old son and a daughter eight years old. Her Christian faith helped her to handle her grief well, and after a few months, she returned to work at the same place where she had worked before her marriage.

She was capable, friendly and still very attractive. Men in and out of the church showed an interest in her, but she held them all at arm's length. She once said she would not remarry until the children were totally on their own. She refused to "inflict" a stepfather on them.

Her busy schedule as breadwinner and single parent sublimated her loneliness. During her children's teen years, they developed friendships and interests outside the home, leaving Joan alone frequently. Slowly, she took on the role of a martyr. Years later, when I (Robert) solemnized the marriage ceremony for her daughter, the world seemed to come to an end for Joan. Her son was away in the Marines, and her daughter married a man who took her to another state to live.

A few months later, Joan told me through her tears that she had been a fool to wrap her whole life in her children by refusing repeated offers of companionship and potential marriage. When I left that community, Joan was frustrated, lonely and very unhappy.

Don't sacrifice your life for what seems like the short-term good of your children. Help them adjust to the coming marriage. Earnestly strive to minimize a sense of competition, concentrating on what they'll gain, not lose, in this coming union. If children are pushed into accepting the new relationship, they will likely resent it. Give them opportunity to build a relationship with your prospective mate. Just as you had time to fall in love, they, too, must fall in love with the new member of the family.

An impending second marriage does present complications, but they can be surmounted. If accepted as challenges and faced squarely, they can strengthen your relationship even before you marry.

Ghosts From the Past

As mentioned earlier, for a second marriage to succeed, former partners must be let go of emotionally. Let's consider how that's done.

The beauty of wedding music and the sacredness of vows will not erase what is in the memory circuits. Buried deep in the recesses of your subconscious lie hidden ghosts of the past that tend to start screaming when you least expect them or want them. They may appear in the bedroom, over a favorite food, during a recreational activity or in the middle of a worship service. Without warning, the person next to you is not your present partner but the person who broke your heart in your former marriage. Your conscious mind tells you it's not true, but your emotions have already reacted to the flashback. More easily than you now believe possible, you will physically, sexually, mentally or spiritually strike out against your present partner because of a past action or attitude of your former partner. You penalize your partner because of a ghost from the past.

You might say, Oh, that would never happen in our lives; we're too much in love! You'd better be in love, but that will not prevent specters from the past. Ghosts will come, and you'll have to deal with them when they do. The quicker you deal with them, the better.

If possible, turn to your partner and say, "I just experienced a flashback, and I'm reacting to it. Such-and-such has happened, and this is what it's doing to me." Talk about it; that's the fastest and best way to get rid of the problem. Ghosts like to live in quiet, undisturbed places. The only way to get them out is to turn the light on and expose them. Talk about them with someone you love, and open the doors and let them fly out of your life. The ghosts may not appear frequently, but your memory will never be erased completely, nor should it; we learn more from our mistakes than from our successes.

Foundations for the Future

Having found a place in God's grace and enjoying a fresh love relationship with a caring member of the opposite sex, it's time to make positive plans for your future. It's time to prove to yourself that you can love again after loss. You're older, more mature and far more capable of handling marital responsibilities if you've dealt with the reasons why your first marriage ended and are walking with the Lord.

Take time to review the five foundations for marriage. Was one or more absent in your previous marriage? The majority of marriages that fail do so because the foundations were not strongly built or maintained.

The imagery we used earlier in the book makes the love you have for each other the "lot" and the marriage the "house" built on that lot. In your case, the first house tumbled. You need to clean up all that rubble and get it out of the way before you start building another house. You won't get rid of every tree and shrub, of course, but you must remove the building blocks from the former house and start all over in building a new one. Many beautiful homes have been built on former home sites. Don't try to use the old material; clean up the old stuff and get rid of it, so you can start fresh.

Since the foundation must precede the construction of the house, begin laying the foundations for your marriage now. You have painfully learned the price of failure. The price of success can't possibly seem too high this time around.

After you have taken your vows and begin the long adjustment necessary to blend two families into one, grow together. Learn together. Share together. Show your concern for each other so that when you reach the apex of your maturity, you will still have a warm relationship going for you.

If you have made the adjustment, put Jesus Christ first and fulfilled the plan of God in your lives, love and be loved! Don't consider yourself second-rate in any way, for what Christ has put under His blood is gone. Live in your new relationship in the fullness of God's grace, and rejoice that the living God in heaven is more interested in your happiness and adjustment to life than you are. Let Him help you build a marriage that this time *will* last till death do you part.

Worksheet

Ken and Kathy's neighbors, Jack and Judy, are both divorced and remarried. Jack has two teenagers who visit every other weekend, and Judy has one ten-year-old child from her previous marriage who lives with her and her new husband.

Jack and Judy, with all three children, came over to Ken and Kathy's house for the day. The plans called for swimming and then a barbecue dinner. As the day progressed, Ken and Kathy noticed that Jack always said yes to his teenagers' requests and no to Judy's daughter's requests. Judy noticed this also, and each time Jack denied a request, she went behind Jack's back and told her child it was OK.

By the end of the day, Jack was swimming in the pool with his children, and Judy was in the house watching TV with her child. Ken and Kathy were at the barbecue pit beginning dinner and wondering how they should handle the situation and the serving of dinner.

1. Should they serve dinner to Judy and her child inside the house and eat outside, as planned, with Jack and his teens?

2. Should they ask Judy and her child to come outside for dinner, hoping the child won't ask Jack for anything?

3. Should they announce to everyone where dinner is going to be served and let nature take its course?

Actually, what Ken and Kathy decide to do about dinner isn't the real problem. Discuss the family dynamics of the blended family.

Who is the rescuer? (mother)

Who is the arbitrary, biased ruler? (father)

Who is the manipulator? (teenagers)

Who is the victim? (ten-year-old)

Could Ken and Kathy help their neighbors by telling them what they've observed? Maybe Jack and Judy need an outside opinion to force them to talk about their problem openly.

PRACTICAL TIPS
FOR PLANNING
YOUR WEDDING DAY

Many of you readers are right now up to your eyeballs in wedding plans. You didn't know it could be so complicated, did you? So many decisions! So many people to please! It can be a time of tension, or it can be a season of getting to know one another better. It's the initial blending of two lives. Do it smoothly.

The earlier you begin your planning, the easier it will be, so don't wait until the last moment. Sit down together and prepare a checklist of things to be done before the wedding day. Then develop a tentative time schedule for each item. If a church wedding is in your plans, check on the availability of the church and the minister very early, for church calendars tend to get overcrowded at certain seasons of the year. Please remember that although your wedding has absolute priority in your life, it may be pretty low in the lives of others. Be aware that religious holidays are difficult seasons to make a church available for a wedding. Recognize also that ministers may have prior commitments that cannot be broken for your wedding. This is equally true of photographers.

As valuable as advice from others can be, never lose sight of the fact that this is *your* wedding. You do not have to compete with the last wedding held in your church, nor is it important for you to do everything the wedding books suggest.

Weddings can be very costly or quite economical. It should go without saying that if you can't pay for it, don't do it. The lavish extras in a big wedding are not worth the price of going deeply into debt. We knew a young couple who insisted upon having a church wedding that was comparable to the most recent lavish celebrations. They ran up such debts that their cars were repossessed, and they couldn't afford a stick of furniture for their apartment—not even a bed—for two years. The wedding was big and beautiful, but the strain that debt put on the couple almost broke up the marriage.

Sometimes the parents of the bride end up deep in wedding-day debt. It doesn't have to be that way. With the help of some friends, some sharp buying and good control on lust levels, a wedding can be beautiful and meaningful without great expense. Simple can be superior.

If the two of you have a limited list of personal friends but would like to have many people witness the wedding, consider having the ceremony at the end of a regular church service. I (Judson) did this as a courtesy to our father's congregation. Parishioners did not have to give up an evening to attend the wedding of their pastor's son.

Whether your wedding is a private or public affair, bridegrooms, recognize that the wedding is the bride's moment of honor. She is the queen, and everything revolves around her. A well-adjusted man will not be threatened by this and will do everything requested of him to make this wedding pageant what his bride longs for it to be. Lifetime memories are being made this day; be certain they're pleasant. His day to be in the spotlight will come, but this is her day.

The final week before the wedding can be unbelievably hectic. Plan, plan and plan to prevent a complete nervous collapse or a disastrous event; then work your plan. You want to enjoy your wedding, not endure it. The better you've prepared, the easier it will be for others to participate. As with most major events, it is far better to be overprepared than underprepared. We'll never forget the wedding that was delayed more than an hour because the minister hadn't arrived. It became evident that the bride thought the bridegroom had contacted him, and the bridegroom assumed the bride had made those arrangements. Since I (Judson) was in the building engaged in another activity, I was pressed into emergency service to perform the ceremony. Bad planning almost prevented this wedding.

Even the best-laid plans can fail somewhere, so expect the unexpected. The ring bearer may drop the rings, the candle lighter may lose the flame on the taper, or the minister may get the names mixed up. In one wedding at which I (Judson) was officiating, a very large bride stepped on the front of her gown on the steps to the platform and fell flat on her face. The bridegroom and I had to maneuver carefully to get her back on her feet. These imperfections are not the end of the world; they're part of the rest of your life. Laugh and keep going. Your marriage is going to need a lot of laughter to lubricate the normal frictions of life.